Companions of Misfortune

Flinders and Friends
at the Isle of France, 1803-1810

Marina Carter

Text: Copyright © Marina Carter, 2003

Photographs: Copyright © Marina Carter, 2003 except images on p. 8, 22, 39, 82, 84 and 108 which were provided courtesy of Genesis Publications Ltd.

The right of Marina Carter to be identified as the author of this work has been asserted by her in accordance with the Copyright, Designs and Patents Act 1988

All rights reserved.

No part of this publication may be reproduced, stored in a retrieval system or transmitted in any form by any means, electronic, mechanical, photocopying, recording or otherwise, except brief extracts for the purpose of review, without the written permission of the copyright owner.

First published in the United Kingdom by
Pink Pigeon Press
92 Greenfield Road
London N15 5ER, UK

ISBN 0-9539916-3-6

Packaged by Next Century Books
P.O.Box 6113
Leighton Buzzard
Bedfordshire LU7 0UW, UK

Printed in India by Gopsons

Contents

Acknowledgements

❖ I would particularly like to thank Marie-France Chelin-Goblet for assisting me with genealogical data

❖ Guy de Richemont, Henri Maurel and Ghyslaine Verdier for providing additional biographical materials

❖ Raymond d'Unienville for advice on French texts

❖ Philippe Lahausse de la Louvière for suggesting this project, and encouraging its completion, and

❖ Luigi di Sarno for assistance with scans and cover design.

❖ Genesis Publications Ltd (www.genesis-publications.com) gave permission to reproduce sketches by G. Ingleton from his book *Matthew Flinders Navigator & Chartmaker*.

❖ I would also like to acknowledge the British Council, the British High Commission, the Société de l'Histoire de l'Ile Maurice, and the Ministry of Tourism of the Government of Mauritius, through the Organising Committee of *Encounter 2003*, for financial support.

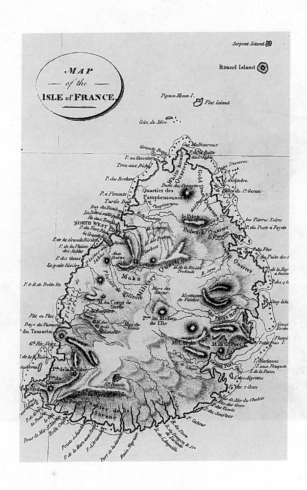

Serpent Island

Round Island

MAP
of the
ISLE of FRANCE.

Pigeon House I.

Flat Island

Coin de Mire

Cap Malheureux

Grande Baye

P. au Piment
Trou aux Biches

P. des Roches

P. à Piments

Baie du Tombeau
Isle aux Tonneliers

NORTH WEST
P. du Port Bon
P. de la Grande Rivière
P. de la Plaine
des Sables
P. des Lianes
La petite Rivière

P. à R. de Belle Ile.

Fabre Baie
aux Cerfs

Pointe Dessous

L'Ambre

Isle de St. Géran

les Pierres Noires
P. du Poste à Fayet

Belu Plac

P. du Puits des

P. de la Bar
à Harine

Idez. 4. G.

Isle

Groso Roche

Flacq

Poste aux I.

L'Marianne
L'aune Fouquets
I. de la Passe

Quartier des
Pamplemousses

Duffe des Pamplem.

Gold Dust

Le Piton

Bubrick Quartier

S. Pierre

Quartier

Ance
Gurne

Mother Quartier

P. de la Rivière
Profonde

R. Jonc

Mare des
Lizards

Moka

Villerre

P. du Corp de
Garde

Pce. du Milieu
de l'Isle

Montagne
de Faïence

TROIS ILOTS

Gf. des
Trois
L'Isleville

Mare aux
Vacois

Plage des
Vacois

Mt. Creole

Mt. du Port

Plac en Plac

Baye du Tamarin
du Tamarin

Gf. Rivr. Noire

P. de la R. Noire

Gf. Riv. Noire

P. du
Coco

Bassin

Grand Port

L. des Négrettes

Pe. de la Mare

I. des 2 Cocos

des Chats

Plaine Cabris de la
Savane

Baie de Mer du Chalon
Mare des Cocos
des Vacois

Pe. du Cap

Pes. de Mer St. Martin
la Prairie

Peros de Mer St. Martin
Belle Côte

Pointe à Sable

P. de la Mare aux aux

Port de Sud

Basin Négresse

P. de la Barre
de la Rivière St. Pe.
de l'Anguille

P. Gabeur

Pe. aux
Sombreux

Introduction

On the 26th September 1803 *Le Berceau* arrived at the Isle of France, bringing news of the rupture of the Peace of Amiens. Only a few weeks later, on 15th December, Flinders appeared off the island, in the *Cumberland*, and sailed into the Baie du Cap. He was to remain a prisoner of the French government there for six and a half years.

Matthew Flinders was returning from a voyage of exploration of the Australian coastline, for which he is today justly celebrated. Fortunately, a remarkable number of the personal and official papers of Flinders have survived, and have been extensively used in the numerous studies published on the life and achievements of this extraordinary naval officer. His lengthy, enforced stay on the island we now know as Mauritius has naturally featured in this literature, which, however is largely devoted to Flinders' own writings and to conveying his personal perspective on the significant events of his life. The intention of the present work is to provide further insights into the circle of friends who surrounded Flinders in Mauritius, and made his confinement and exile on the island more bearable. Ly Tio Fane's 1988 study of Flinders' years spent at the Isle of France provides a detailed account of the whys and wherefores of his extended time in captivity, which is therefore not rehashed here. Instead, the primary focus of this volume is the investigation of the 'companions of misfortune' encountered by Flinders at the Isle of France, and the distractions and occupations which engaged and comforted him.

Flinders' habit of copying letters and keeping a daily journal, and the care taken of these documents by those who carried them back to England, and others who conserved them as family heirlooms have provided his biographers with a rich legacy. The painstaking perusal of their contents not only reveals the humanity of Flinders and of those who surrounded him, but offers a unique record of the impact of the Napoleonic wars in a French colonial outpost. The documents are quoted as seen, with spellings and occasional linguistic idiosyncracies unchanged. Translations of the brief French texts, and summaries of the longer quotations are provided at the end of the book. French place-names went in and out of fashion, according to Revolutionary tastes, and for the sake of simplicity the two ports of the Isle of France are termed Port Louis and Grand Port throughout. The two Mascarene islands are usually described according to their 18th century names – Bourbon and Isle of France, however after 1810, the latter was renamed Mauritius, and this change is noted in the text and used thereafter.

The explorer narrative is a distinctive form of historical writing, in which the author often aims "not to record history but to make it – to establish his own historical significance" [Carter: 91-2]. There was little attempt at objectivity in Flinders' narrative, upon which we cannot therefore rely for a balanced account of General Decaen's actions, for example. Yet this in no way diminishes its historical significance. Australia's explorer narratives, including that of Flinders

> *do not proceed smoothly towards the longed-for denouement
> …but consist of a multitude of fragmentary asides, speculative
> observations, scraps of dialogue, reminiscences which struggle
> inconclusively for definition and dominance* [Carter: 106].

The value of Matthew Flinders' letters, and journal, and the correspondence addressed to him, lies precisely in the refreshingly different view of events he provides for us, as compared to the standard histories of the time.

It is into this treasure trove of letters and narratives, stored in archives spanning three continents, that the present work dips, to describe the uncertainties of war and the importance of propaganda on an isolated island, and to provide new and personal insights into some of the dramatic battles and events of the Napoleonic Wars in the Indian Ocean. Above all, the individual accounts cited reveal the human stories that are part of every conflict, and which so often belie the hostility and

2

deadly antagonisms of the larger political landscape. The supreme irony of men who were enemies at sea and friends on shore is laid bare, and Flinders' own perspective underscored:

What an age are we born in! ... The thirst of conquest or the necessity of repulsing aggression have converted the plough shares of England and France into swords, and the useful arts of peace are made to give way, or only considered as subservient to the destructive art of war. The little path that I had traced out to myself, by which to arrive at some distinction, had nothing to recommend it but its philanthropic principles and its general utility to commerce and the extension of natural, geographical, and nautical knowledge; these are become antiquated themes amidst the violent commotions that agitate distracted Europe.

On the Isle of France, at least, Flinders could feel that these 'antiquated themes' were given their due recognition.

In fact Flinders received his first offers of help from French officers actively engaged in making war against his compatriots, and it was to a serving French naval ensign – Charles Baudin – that he expressed his appreciation for the esteem and support of his companions in misfortune:

That the sentiments of men the most capable of appreciating what I have done and what I have suffered, are universally in my favour, has been, and is the greatest consolation ... a restoration to liberty even without that would to me lose its greatest charm.

Flinders was fortunate to encounter a number of remarkable and talented individuals on the Isle of France and cultivated a wide circle of acquaintances during his years on the island. There were military men – like Jacques Plumet who had served native Indian princes against the British; intellectuals – like the scientists and artists who disembarked from Baudin's expedition and remained on the island; colonial landed proprietors – some descended from French noble families; and men of learning and gentility who encompassed all of the above, like Barthelemy Huet de Froberville, a former officer and a savant, who had written the first novel of the region, and had made extensive studies of Madagascar. At times Flinders felt that if only his wife could be with him, he could be happy for an indefinite period on the island. In a letter to his brother Samuel, written in December 1806, a list of his Isle of France acquaintances was given:

My most particular friends are, first, the family of Madame d'Arifat with whom I reside, consisting of a widow lady, three sons and three daughters; second, Mr. Thomas Pitot, a young man of considerable abilities and a most excellent heart: he is a merchant in the town, in partnership with his uncle and elder brother, and is secretary to the literary Society of Emulation commenced here by the men of science left here by M. Baudin; third the family and extensive friends of Mr. Pitot; fourth, all the relations and friends of the family d'Arifat, are my friends more or less, and anxious well wishers, particularly M. Froberville their cousin and the intimate friend of Mr. Pitot: Mr. F. is a member of the society, an author, and a long time editor of the public gazette; and he, as well as Mr. Pitot and his brother are musicians, fifth, Mons. Charles Baudin, ensign de vaisseau on board la Piémontaise frigate: he was a midshipman on board Le Géographe; and lastly our near neighbours Messieurs Chazal and Chevreau, married to two sisters; they are both respectable habitants, or planters and the former has been in England, is an excellent painter, and a man of strong sense: his lady is the first performer on the harpsichord in the I. of France, and I often accompany her with my flute.

It has been well said that "friendships were integral to Matthew Flinders' life. He made friends easily, and retained them" [Brunton: 18-19]. The importance of his island companions may be surmised by Flinders' own words on the subject of friendship, made in a letter to Thomi, which he called "the almost indescribable communion of mind, the similarity of sentiments and of taste, and that jumping together of the heart upon occasions that call forth the feelings of humanity". Indeed, Flinders made so many new friends on the island that when he was finally allowed to leave, his heart was 'oppressed' at the prospect of leaving them, probably for good.

Certainly, the friendships cultivated by Flinders while on the Isle of France, as he himself frequently acknowledged, were of immense importance in enabling him to remain in good spirits, and productive, during his years of incarceration. It is noteworthy that the crowning achievement of his life – the chart of 'Terra Australis' – was completed on Mauritius. Flinders always believed that his calling, and that of intellectuals and scientists worldwide, outshone and would outlive the gains and setbacks of war as a letter to Charles Baudin revealed:

> *The labours of Newton and Cook were beneficial, whilst those of Alexander and Caesar desolated mankind. Would that our two nations were convinced of this truth, and act accordingly, then might we hope the animosity which makes it a duty for one man to destroy another, would become an honourable emulation for excellence in the useful arts and sciences.*

Fortunately, the savants and litterati he cultivated in Mauritius amply demonstrated by their actions that intellectual curiosity and fellowship could far outweigh any enmities that might have been nurtured by misplaced notions of patriotic duty.

The story of Flinders' relationships with his fellow prisoners and ostensible enemies reveals that even in the grimmest moments of war, acts of common humanity are not only possible but acquire a significance which can override many of the injustices and privations suffered. Whilst the era of officers' parole and gentlemanly codes of conduct has long passed, the individuals who illuminate this narrative offer a salutary lesson in this modern era of global warfare and terrorism.

Baie du Cap – where Flinders first arrived

My mission, as was Baudin's was for peace,
To further science and explore,
This should, in alien eyes my fame increase,
No part had I in wasteful war

This island, far removed, an alien soil,
Displayed much beauty to my searching eyes,
Rich flora, harvests for so little toil
A land of storm and cloud, and azure skies

Six years and six long months I'd captive been
Then on June seventh I left that tropic isle:
Land of the Dodo, mist and saffron-green,
Where valued friendships tempered my exile.
Beard, W. *Navigator Immortal*, 1958.

PART ONE

ONE

Comrades
in Exile

"all the people of the earth constitute the family of a navigator"
Matthew Flinders to Charles Baudin

The Café Marengo, at the port
[as visualized by Geoffrey Ingleton]

A View of Port Louis, c. 1812

Compatriots and Prisoners

Shortly after his arrival at the Isle of France, Flinders was transferred to the first of several establishments which would serve as his prisons over succeeding years. He and John Aken, master of the *Cumberland*, were taken to a "very dirty tavern of Port Louis", as Flinders described it, where the men spent an uncomfortable night "besieged by swarms of bugs and musketoes". The Café Marengo, according to the navigator, was "a large house in the middle of the town", and here Flinders was to spend his first hundred days on the island, in company with Aken, and another seaman, John Elder, former master-at-arms aboard the *Investigator*, and employed as Flinders' servant at the Isle of France. These men, along with other Englishmen who would subsequently share his incarceration, became Flinders' first circle of friends on the island.

1. Shipmates

The *Cumberland* was a small vessel, and Flinders had only a handful of crew with him when he arrived at the Isle of France in December 1803. While Aken and himself lodged at the Café Marengo, the seamen from the *Cumberland* were confined on a guard ship, from where, Flinders reported at the end of January 1804, one man, Francis Smith - a Prussian former convict - had run away in a Spanish frigate, the officers of which had also attempted to persuade John Wood and Henry Lewis to go with them. Their conditions were not happy: prevented from walking on shore, they "were kept strictly on board the prison ship, and locked up every night. No clothes were supplied to them", remarked Flinders. In March he was allowed to speak to Edward Charrington, his boatswain, and asked him to keep an eye on the rest of the crew.

Shortly afterwards, the men were transferred to a prison in Flacq, on the eastern side of the island, while Flinders, Aken and Elder remained in the western port capital. Flinders thus saw very little of the other members of the *Cumberland* during his time in captivity. In the early days, however, both Aken and Elder were a source of much comfort to Flinders. Elder, in particular, became the eyes and ears of his master – sent out to the bazaar each day, he attempted to gain information about ship movements, and to make any other contacts that he considered might be useful to Flinders. Aware that the navigator was curious about the voyage of their French rivals from the *Géographe*, for example, one day he made the acquaintance of a seaman who had served on that vessel and was consequently able to give Flinders a detailed account of the movements of the French ship after Baudin's departure from Port Jackson. In July 1804 Elder was also sent on board the prison ship to enquire after George Alder, who had been kept in irons there. Alder was given permission by Flinders to board the *Psyché* frigate, in order to obtain some spending money, on condition that he was not carried to sea in her.

Meanwhile, after 4 months in the Café, Flinders and his companions were transferred to the Maison Despeaux, where "we had a piece of ground to walk in, and the society of several of our countrymen", as the navigator reported. In August 1804 Flinders requested that Alder be allowed to join them there, as a servant to Aken, but in September his boatswain, Charrington, was one of a number of men who escaped from their confinement at Flacq to the English frigates then cruising off the island. Flinders later heard that Charrington and 6 others had seized a boat "and got without side of the reef before they could be overtaken, either by the shot of the field pieces, or by the boats sent after them". As a result, a stricter regime was instituted for the remaining English prisoners who were marched to a converted hospital serving as a prison at Grand River. Flinders saw them pass the gate of the Garden Prison "under a strong guard". At that prison, which consisted essentially of two rooms, the seamen were shut up in the lower, and the officers in the upper apartments. Flinders was later to receive several complaints from the *Cumberland's* mariners who were given no clothes and little to eat there. One seaman, suffering from dysentery, was sent to the hospital, where he joined Aken, who had also fallen ill. In December another member of the crew managed to escape.

Elder was unfailingly described by Flinders as "faithful and attentive', while John Aken, in letters to his wife, was characterized as "an easy, good-natured man", "and earnest to do all he can for my relief". In May 1805 Flinders was surprised and pleased to learn from Aken that he had been given permission to leave the island on an American ship. On 18th May, he boarded the *James*, bound for New York, carrying with him papers and charts relating to the voyage of the *Investigator*, and letters from Flinders to the Admiralty Office and others in England. George Alder also went home on the same ship, along with several other English prisoners and 30 French passengers. John Wood and Henry Lewis having left on the American ship *Brutus*, and James Carter, on the *Lobere*, by July there remained on the island from the *Cumberland* besides Elder and Flinders, only William Smith. He was recovering from a broken leg, and Flinders made a request to the local authorities to keep the man with him, rather than sending him away on a cartel. Elder also continued to serve Flinders – as the latter wrote in a letter to his wife dated 7th July 1805: "I gave him his choice to go away with the other prisoners in the cartel, but he seems determined to stay by me, until we shall weather this storm of adversity".

The departed Aken was not forgotten, and in his loneliness, Flinders even addressed him a letter, suggesting that he might consider returning to the island to chaperone Ann Flinders. To his wife, however, Flinders complained, in June 1807, of having no news from Mr Aken, "who has left many things untold, of which he should have given me information". When Aken left the Isle of France, he had been given a letter of recommendation by Flinders which described him as a "sober, careful and trusty officer", well informed in matters of navigation, and "a proper person to take charge of a merchant ship". It was indeed in that capacity that Aken was subsequently employed, for in 1812,

Flinders informed a mutual friend: "Mr. Aken is now in the West Indies, commanding a fine merchant ship".

Flinders also gave Aken news of his *Cumberland* shipmates, informing him that he had obtained permission for Smith to embark on board the *Martha Clarke*, bound for Boston, but that Elder stayed on. In April 1806, Flinders had written of Elder: "I shall never part with him until he parts with me", but within a short time, he was reporting that his servant had become depressed and paranoid. Finally Elder asked for permission to leave, which was granted, and in July 1807 he departed for Baltimore on an American brig, supplied with certificates for the attention of His Majesty's naval officers, in which Flinders testified to his 'diligence and sobriety'. He was also described in them as faithful, attentive, and honest, and Flinders added "I have always placed the greatest confidence in his integrity and have never once had reason to repent it". There was an unmistakable sincerity in his closing lines, "I have complied with his long delayed request to obtain a permission for him to leave this island, although in so doing I lose a most valuable servant and assistant whom I wish well with all my heart and wish it was in my power to serve". Later, after his own return to England, Flinders received many enquiries from Mauritian friends concerning his unfortunate servant, and was able to report that Elder had been appointed 'master at arms' and in 1812 was serving with Rear Admiral Hollowell in the Mediterranean.

2. Compatriot POWs

During the first months of his confinement in the capital, first at the Café Marengo and then at the Maison Despeaux, Flinders also found much solace in the company of his fellow prisoners of war. In late February 1804 he learned from the interpreter that an Indiaman, the *Admiral Aplin*, had been brought in as a prize, and sent Elder to communicate with "the officers and their ladies" who had been passengers on board. A number of them were lodged at the Garden Prison along with Dale and Seymour, two midshipmen of the *Dédaigneuse*. Alfred Dale was to provide

12

Flinders with much assistance in his chart-making, and when he left was issued with the following certificate:

on April 1 1804 when I was removed to the Garden Prison in this island, I found here Mr. Alfred Dale midshipman of His Majestys ship Dedaigneuse. From that time to the date hereof, being one year and one hundred days, he has given me assistance in making astronomical calculations, and has made copies of charts relating to my voyage of discovery which have been transmitted to the Lords Commissioners of the Admiralty.

During 1804, each month brought new arrivals from the prizes captured by the privateers, while others were given permission to leave for home via America or India. As Flinders noted in his *Voyage to Terra Australis* "a prisoner or two were occasionally added to our number from the prizes brought in; but when amounting to 6 or 8, they were marched off to join the other merchant officers at Flacq". Flinders recorded the movements on and off the island of English prisoners in some detail, and, with an eye on his own predicament, frequently looked for signs or patterns in the treatment of the POWs which might indicate a softening of official attitudes.

The departure of fellow prisoners occasioned mixed emotions for Flinders as he noted in his journal: "Mr. Robertson left us this afternoon. I suffer the loss of an agreeable companion in him, and of a well-informed good man, but rejoice sincerely in his liberty". Indeed, in a letter to his wife, he wrote that the society of his compatriots had helped to restore him to good health. There was one benefit to being the solitary prisoner left, however: Flinders was assured that greater freedom would be granted to him, following the departure of the numerous POWs on the island. Thus, after the cartel had carried away his friends, midshipmen Dale and Seymour, together with most of those incarcerated at the Grand River prison, Flinders was allowed to leave the capital to reside on an upland estate.

Wherever he was on the island, however, Flinders treasured the contacts, whether verbal or written, which he was able to maintain with his compatriots. They were not simply a source of practical assistance and emotional sustenance, but a link to the outside world. He frequently addressed letters to the cartels and to arriving officers to request intelligence of the war, and copies of newspapers and other published materials.

Flinders also followed with interest the skirmishes and pitched sea battles that preceded the arrival of prisoners, as far as he could glean the details. In July 1806, for example, he recounted the clash between the *Warren Hastings* and *La Piémontaise*, which resulted in the deaths of 12 men and the capture of the Indiaman's Chinese cargo valued at $600,000. He reported that the prize's arrival in Grand Port

> *formed a topic of conversation for the whole island. The defence that Captain Larkins made, even according to the French account was very honourable to the commander and company, more so than the treatment they afterwards received ... for it was said that owing to a mistake on board the Piémontaise frigate, that the Warren Hastings was trying to run them down after having struck, they boarded her in fury and wounded the captain and some others who made no resistance.*

The officers and men of the *Warren Hastings* were taken to the Grand River prison; later Larkins was given permission to stay at the home of a colonist in Flacq, where he received a letter from Flinders, who commiserated with Larkins for the loss of his ship, commended his "gallant action" and offered his thanks, "for having so well sustained the honour of our country". Flinders' chief object was to request information of "our country and its affairs". Larkins had himself been away from home for a year and a half, but was able to provide some news about mutual acquaintances and former shipmates.

Larkins' departure in late July 1806 gave Flinders the chance to transmit a copy of the narrative of his voyage to the Admiralty Office in London. Other departing prisoners provided useful opportunities to send letters to England or India. In the middle of 1807, he had hopes that he would be able to depart on the *Wellesley* cartel then in the port, having learnt of instructions from France directing his release. But, once again, with the sailing of the cartel, Flinders realised, "I shall again see myself the only English prisoner in the Isle of France: I who never did or intended any kind of warfare".

During 1808, Flinders was able to interact by letter and in person with a number of other POWS, including Captain Richardson of the *Althea*, and Captain Woolcombe of the *Laurel*, whose action with the *Cannonière* was said to have "excited the admiration of the captors". In September, he went to discuss his prospects of leaving the island – clandestinely or otherwise – with Woolcombe, but reported: "the captain received me very coldly, did not think I ought to consider myself disengaged from parole; had torn the letter received from me, and did not intend to give any answer". Notwithstanding, Flinders addressed a second letter to Woolcombe, offering his services, "either in furnishing or procuring you money should you have occasion for it, or in any other way that you conceive my experience and acquaintance in the island can be useful for although I have the misfortune of differing in opinion with you upon a certain point, this can be no reason with me for not desiring to be useful to a countryman in misfortune".

In November 1808, Flinders also addressed a letter to another POW, Captain Henry Lynne, from whom he had obtained an Admiralty List, regretting that it would not be possible for the captain to visit him in his inland retreat: "the almost entire deprivation of the society of my countrymen for many years past does not certainly tend to diminish my desire of communicating with them". In March 1809, Lynne was still awaiting permission to leave the island, and considering resorting to bribery. The notion intrigued Flinders, who wrote in reply: "I am curious to learn the negotiation of which you speak; if you succeed by bribery, and see any possibility that the same means might procure for me the same advantage … will you be so good as to make an offer for five-hundred dollars on my part for a permission to quit the island". Evidently Lynne's plan did not work out, for in August 1809, he remained a prisoner, and

Flinders, for his part, confided that his own project of concealing himself aboard a departing cartel had been rejected as impracticable. He had nevertheless informed Admiral Bertie by letter, that "I no longer consider myself to be upon parole, and have given him my reasons for it; which if he approves, he will perhaps order to be put into execution a plan I have proposed, for withdrawing myself from the unjust hand which has so long oppressed me".

By this stage of his confinement, it was evident that Flinders considered his fellow POWs to be useful sounding boards for his plans of escape. Evidently he and Lynne had worked out an elaborate code by which a visiting British ship would signal to Flinders, in order to enable him to effect his escape, for in a further letter to Lynne, details were outlined of the prospective departure arrangements:

if the ship wears her pendant forward, - if when she lies to, it is with the fore topsail to the mast, - and when under sail, if her main royal or top-gallant sail are set, and the fore royal or top-gallant sail are in, I should be still more certain that my plan was adopted and the execution about to take place: you will remember high-water, and day break or a little before. Should the ship see any person upon or near the shore, with a white handkerchief constantly in his left hand, she will know that I see and understand what is preparing.

In the event, the dramatic escape attempt would not be made, and Flinders would leave, at last, with the approbation of the Captain General, Decaen.

While Woolcombe had given Flinders a cool reception, another English officer, R.P. Brereton, midshipman of the *Sea Flower*, proved a disagreeable acquaintance of another sort. He addressed Flinders a letter in 1809, claiming to be a relative, to which the navigator responded positively, sending him fifty dollars. He was soon made aware that Brereton was a man of no good character, and the commander of the *Sea Flower*, Lieutenant Owen, offered to refund the sum that Flinders had advanced to the midshipman. Flinders characteristically responded that the sum could be used to meet any debts which Brereton might have on the island, and which "I should wish for the honour of our country to be liquidated before that to me is thought of". The incident did, however, prove to be the means of introducing Flinders to Owen, who would become a firm friend.

In November 1809 the *Henrietta* cartel arrived from Bengal. On board were Mr Ramsden, a former prisoner in the Maison Despeaux, and commander of the vessel, and the Commissary of Prisoners, Mr Hope. This was to be the means by which Flinders would leave the island, though some time and much correspondence would ensue before this was finally effected. On 18th December Flinders addressed Hope with his usual request: "I need scarcely observe to you, Sir, how much I shall be obliged by your using your endeavours to obtain my release from this island". Hope responded, on 23rd December, as follows:

I am perfectly acquainted with all the circumstances relating to you and you may rest assured that it is my anxious desire as it must be of every Englishman to obtain the liberty of a person so unjustly detained and who has rendered such services to his country.... I have been received with the greatest attention by the General and although I should be sorry to raise expectations which might afterwards be disappointed, I confess, my hopes are great...As I am pretty narrowly watched do not mention that you heard from me.

Hope urged Flinders not to be impatient, as he did not wish to be unduly rushed in his plans for Flinders' release. It was not until March 1810, in fact, that the happy news was imparted by Hope, who rejoiced "in being the means of restoring to his friends, his family and his country a man so worthy of their esteem and admiration". From his conversations with Monistrol, Hope gathered that Flinders would be required not to bear arms, and asked for his views, to which the navigator replied that he was prepared to agree to this, which would thus preclude him from taking part "in any expedition against the Isle of France", but he positively refused to consider dining with the Governor: "I can never enter the government house as a guest, and I much

17

desire and hope that the general will not lay me, a second time, under the necessity of refusing him". Flinders, at this point, could not even bring himself to imagine meeting Colonel Monistrol, despite that officer's friendly dealings with him, fearing that he might not be able to hold his temper in check.

Quite how Hope arranged for Flinders' release, when so many had failed, is unknown. But he certainly had greater bargaining power: the island was abuzz with rumours of an English attack, and Decaen was no doubt already considering his options. Eight months later, when Britain did indeed take the island, Decaen was treated exceptionally favourably. In any event, Flinders was shortly afterwards able to take his departure, and soon transferred off the ship, so as to return to England via the Cape rather than India.

General Decaen   *Admiral Bertie*

At the Cape, Flinders found Admiral Bertie preparing for the expedition against the islands, and provided that officer with intelligence concerning the island and the layout of the port. He socialized little with the Admiral, however, finding him "reserved and so little polite". Bertie, on the other hand, seems to have been well disposed toward Flinders. After the conquest, he himself searched the Engineer's office for Flinder's journal, and protested to General Abercrombie at Decaen's having been allowed to remove it from the colony [Mack: 222].

Meanwhile, Flinders' fellow prisoners, including Lieutenant William F. Owen, had journeyed on to India, from where Flinders received news of their progress. Owen sent a genial note on 1st August, from his retreat near Madras, in terms which indicated the level of intimacy which had developed between himself and Flinders: "you cannot doubt how much our little society missed you - we toasted you, Sir, like Englishmen". Reporting that they had "a very agreeable voyage", Owen confessed, that "the charms of one young lady rendered it particularly so to me. I could have worshipped the little witch for life; but fate, or in your philosophic language, the general laws by which the universe is governed, seem to have denied me this indulgence". The romance, and the reason for its abrupt termination, were clarified in a letter sent by Hope to Flinders in October 1810:

> We arrived at Madras the 7th of July without any remarkable occurrence save Owen's losing his heart to Miss Butler. ... I stopt only 3 days at Madras to land the prisoners and take some fresh water on board. Owen was obliged to remain at Madras to his great regret and allow his flame to proceed on to Bengal. I was received by Lord Minto in the most gracious manner and all my arrangements were approved.

Back in England, Flinders was able to renew his acquaintance with former friends, including some of his fellow prisoners at Mauritius. In April 1811, he was visited by John Aken, who was en route to Jamaica, and learnt that Alfred Dale had been promoted to second lieutenant on the *Belle Poule*. Owen kept in regular contact by mail. It was he who chased up Flinders' trunk, found in Bengal by Hope "with its contents half eaten by white ants" and provided regular news of mutual friends. Hugh Hope also sent news from India of their former shipmates and their lady friends: "my favourite little Miss Butler is the only one unmarried of all ours and she might have had our Messmate Owen had he pleased her taste".

19

Owen himself had a score or two to settle, having evidently been told some tall tales by his fellow prisoners at the Isle of France, as he jovially informed Flinders:

> *I met old Lynne in the Eclipse and find you were right, he never met you at Mauritius, by jove he lied when in prison, but prison tales should not be taken for orthodox or gospel. ... When we met I was not only his superior but his commodore. My stars what a chance for retaliating injury! I did so. ... but I hate to humble a man I like at all and who can say he has no failings? His were a little vanity - mine may be something worse.*

In June 1813, Owen took advantage of home leave to call upon Flinders in London, and the following year, after his friend's death, offered his services to Ann. William Fitzwilliam Owen would go on to become an admiral, and a distinguished hydrographic surveyor – in many respects, achieving what Flinders might have looked forward to become, had he lived longer. Ironically, also, it was Owen who had the opportunity to return to Mauritius– in 1824 – spending 8 weeks there. And, the island that had before been for him a 'hell-hole' and a 'dungeon' was now, he wrote, "gifted with every blessing and beauty that nature's most lavish hand could bestow". How Flinders would have revelled in that chance of a return visit!

Officers and Gentlemen

I n Port Louis, after a brief, fatal encounter with the Captain-General, Decaen, it would be chiefly through his aide-de-camp, Louis Auguste Fulcher de Monistrol, assisted by the interpreter, François Dominique Bonnefoy, that Flinders would interact. From the outset he noted that the French officials sent to perform Decaen's orders behaved in a sympathetic manner towards him. They, along with a number of French military officers, would prove to be a source of moral support and practical assistance during Flinders' imprisonment.

Flinders received his first taste of island hospitality at the home of Major d'Unienville after his arrival at the Baie du Cap, in the *Cumberland*. He had followed a schooner through the reefs, and, noting that its occupants became agitated, surmised that his nation was again at war with France. According to the report made by the French major to Decaen on that day, 15 December 1803, and conserved in the French archives, on seeing the English vessel, he sounded the alarm, called some of the national guard to his aid, armed his plantation slaves, and ordered the women and children into the woods with the animals. He then made his way to the coastal fortifications, and seeing that the *Cumberland* had only a few people on board, hailed them to send their canoe, and visited the ship, whereupon Flinders introduced himself, stating that he had not intended to excite alarm, being unaware that the two nations were again at war.

The journal kept by Flinders gives several reasons for this fateful decision to stop at the Isle of France: chief of them were that the Cumberland was leaking, and needed its 'upper works caulked', wood and water were wanted, and a 'small supply of spiritis', and – ironically – it was hoped that a homeward bound ship which could offer "a more expeditious and convenient passage to England" might be found there [Ingleton: 259].

The navigator's journal records that Monsieur d'Unienville "entertained me very politely", offered the crew fresh fruit, and:

> *did not let his hospitality rest here... but pressed me to dine at his house where he invited several of the neighbouring gentlemen ... our friendly party, ladies and all, attended me to the shore and sent off a basket of mangos with other refreshments. Monsieur le Citoyen Dunienville and his lady seem to be indeed amiable people.*

At the time of Flinders' arrival, d'Unienville lived with his wife, Hortense de Barry, and two year old son, on his small estate 'Choisy', near the bay.

Major d'Unienville

The Cumberland [by Ingleton]

It was also from Major d'Unienville that Flinders learnt the fate of fellow explorer Nicolas Baudin. The Frenchman had preceded him by a few months – arriving at the island on 7 August 1803, but had died on 16th September, and was interred there.

The next day, Flinders was ordered to the capital and went to meet Decaen. After the *Cumberland's* arrival at the port, Flinders received a cool reception at government house. He later described General Decaen as "a shortish thick man in a laced round jacket" and the aide-de-camp as a person of a more tranquil appearance. Flinders certainly found the latter a more sympathetic figure, and was soon benefiting from his helpful advice. As early as 27 December 1803, for example, Monistrol warned Flinders that his method of dealing with Decaen had not been helpful. The Englishman confided in his journal "Mr Monistrol appeared very sorry that I had written to the general in the stile that I had done". At the same time Flinders was consoled by the interpreter's "conviction of the propriety of my cause". Bonnefoy and the surgeon, Chapotin, visited the navigator every other day during January 1804.

Around this time, aware that the English prisoners were in want of money, Bonnefoy also arranged a transaction that surprised Flinders. The Danish consul, the Chevalier Charles de Pelgrom, offered to cash their bills at par, leaving Flinders to confess to his journal "in the present transaction I find myself much indebted to the Chevalier and the Interpreter".

At the Café Marengo, however, it was Jacques Bergeret, a French naval officer turned privateer, whose friendship and offers of help were to provide a lifeline to a confused and angry Flinders. On 10 February 1804, Flinders reported the visit of Bergeret who:

> sat some time and conversed upon my situation which he seemed desirous to ameliorate, and was kind enough to point out to me the most probable mode of bringing this about. He offered to supply my want of money if any existed.

Captain Bergeret, then in command of the privateer *La Psyché* was known to be a man of honour and humanity. Having just captured the *Admiral Aplin*, he had successfully pleaded for the British army officers on board and their wives to lodge in a tavern at the capital. Bergeret's privileged access to Decaen soon also procured beneficial results for Flinders. On 31st May 1804 he arranged for Flinders to be transferred to the 'garden prison'. The Maison Despeaux was a large house, with a walled garden, several acres in size. Flinders described the house as 'airy' and 'agreeable', and stated that it had been built by a surgeon and formerly used as a gaming house, and to lodge the ambassadors sent by Tipu Sultan to the island in 1798.

As a confidant of Decaen, Bergeret was necessarily privy to views on both sides that it would have been unwise to communicate. At this time Flinders was still clinging to the notion of securing a patron who could arrange his speedy return to Europe and Bergeret warned him, for example, not to expect too much. Flinders nevertheless addressed a letter to Admiral Linois in mid April 1804, shortly after that officer's arrival on the island. The Admiral unsuccessfully appealed to be authorized to take Flinders with him to France aboard the *Marengo*, as did Captain Halgan of *Le Berceau* who also visited Flinders and offered him money and assistance. Linois was at least able to deliver a letter from Flinders to one of Nicholas Baudin's lieutenants on the *Géographe*, Captain Milius. Flinders' amicable relationship with Linois did not prevent him from congratulating his brother for his part in "driving off the French admiral Linois", referring to Samuel's role in defence of the China fleet when the French under Linois attacked during February 1804.

Admiral Linois   *Linois' ship, the Marengo, in battle*

By June 1804, Flinders was writing of Bergeret as a 'friend' and reported that he had asked the Frenchman to intercede again with Decaen, this time to obtain permission to reside in the country. The Governor rejected the request but Bergeret's support was acknowledged in Flinders' journal:

From this gentleman a great number of English prisoners have received kindnesses. The situations of some he has bettered, to others he has advanced money, and for others he has obtained permission to depart from hence. He deserves the thanks of every

24

Englishman who wishes well to his countrymen and countrywomen in misfortune.

In his first letter to his wife from the island dated July 1804, after detailing his misadventures, Flinders also recorded his debt to Captain Bergeret, who had just helped to secure the return of his books and charts, indicating that the captain's "good heart' went some way towards mitigating the effect of Decaen's animosity.

Soon afterwards, in a letter to his brother, Flinders reported that he had made the acquaintance of another ship's captain – Augustin Baudin, brother of explorer Nicolas Baudin. Flinders described him as "exceedingly kind and civil" and was gratified to learn that Nicolas had mentioned in glowing terms the attention and assistance he had received from English governor King and his officers at the Port Jackson colony. Augustin reported that the letter had been published in the Madras newspapers, and Flinders added, "Captain Baudin appeared to be fully sensible of the great difference in my treatment, and deprecated it very much". Augustin, having left the French service, was then in command of a Danish ship from Tranquebar, and on 19 August 1804, on the eve of his return to India, he paid another visit to Flinders, to wish him goodbye, and to consult him on the question of Mary Beckwith – the young woman brought by his brother from Australia, to where she had been transported as a convict, for a petty theft when aged only 14. Unfortunately, Flinders left no details of the advice he must have offered Baudin, but it is believed that Mary left with Augustin when he returned to Tranquebar in that year.

Within a few days, Flinders was obliged to bid adieu to another of his friends – Jacques Bergeret – who was about to leave on a cruise in the *Psyché*. This frigate was a former privateer purchased by Decaen in autumn 1804 for the use of the French government, of which Linois decided to keep Bergeret, "her brave and enterprising captain", in command. The *Psyché* took several prizes before succumbing to a superior force. A contemporary naval account reported that the *St Fiorenzo*, a British frigate commanded by Henry Lambert had gone in search of Bergeret's ship, reported to be off Vizagapatam, catching up with the French frigate, and engaging her in combat for several hours. The *Psyché* was no match for the *St Fiorenzo* but put up a spirited resistance, until, with more than half of the crew killed or wounded, Bergeret struck his flag "out of humanity to the survivors of his crew". The British account recorded this tribute to Bergeret: "every Frenchman, who wishes well to the navy of his country, should hold in honourable recollection the heroic defence of the Psyché". When news filtered through of the event, Flinders commented approvingly: "it appears that he has been treated in the most handsome manner, both by the naval officers in India and by the Marquis Wellesley".

A French 'capitaine de vaisseau'

Interior of a French warship

Flinders had complained, following their last meeting, that Bergeret "is mighty costive in giving any intelligence of the squadron or other matters interesting to us", and confided to Joseph Banks, that a letter written to Fleurieu on his behalf by Admiral Linois, was "a cautious one". However, the dangers of loose talk were only too evident: the interpreter, Bonnefoy, was dismissed in October 1805, reportedly for passing on copies of a journal which gave an account of a sea battle involving Linois. Flinders wrote: "Bonnefoy it seems did not enter into the General's views of monopolizing all intelligence". And Linois himself was no longer in the good graces of Decaen: in November 1804 Thomi Pitot had addressed Flinders a short note – evidently written hurriedly as the English was not of his usual high standard – which stated:

I cannot more depend upon the very favourable disposition of the General Linois in your favour. New misintelligency ... have taken room yesterday between the Captain General and him and I see with the greatest pain that his mediation would be more noxious than useful to your interest.

The return of Bergeret, with a number of other French prisoners in a cartel, the *Thetis*, in June 1805, nevertheless gave Flinders some hope of being allowed to leave in her, particularly when he learned from the captain of the cartel that his French friend had applied to Decaen for his release in exchange for himself. Once again, however, Decaen allowed others to depart, while retaining Flinders. A separate request by Bergeret to the Captain General was acceded to, however, and in the middle of August Flinders was permitted to move to the interior of the island. Acting on advice from friends, Flinders selected the residence of Mme d'Arifat in Plaines Wilhems, leaving his town prison in August 1805. Bergeret accompanied him on a visit to Monistrol to finalise the details of his parole.

In his new abode, Flinders was able to enlarge his circle of acquaintances. One of his first invitations was to the estate of Jacques Plumet, situated between the Terre Rouge and Mesnil rivers. Flinders described him as "a respectable inhabitant who had formerly been an officer in the Mahratta service, and commanded in some successful actions against our forces in the East Indies". Plumet is known to have been one of several Frenchmen who drilled European-style armies for the benefit of independent Indian states in the late 18th century.

By 1793, the French had lost all their possessions in India to the British. Yet, they not only continued to menace merchant shipping from their Mascarene base, but also to pose a threat from within India, through their political alliances and military support to the local princes.

Major Lewis Ferdinand Smith, one of the few contemporaries of Captain Plumet to have left a written record of this extraordinary page of Indian military history, described him as a "Frenchman and a gentleman; two qualities which were seldom united in the Mahratta army" and a man of "respectable character and sound principles". In June 1801, Plumet commanded several regular battalions for Jeswant Rao Holkar in an attack on a rival Maratha force marshalled under the command of Major George Hessing at Ujain, and at the encounter between Jaswant Rao's troops and two battalions commanded by Major Brownrigg in July 1801. This second battle was described as follows:

Jaswant Rao arrived in great strength and had with him the good Major Plumet and a brigade of regular infantry ... After some hours of facing the swarms of case-shot sent hissing into the packed files by fifty massed guns, and the volleys and the immovable hedge of bayonets of the infantry even Plumet's regulars could not be induced to make yet another attack.
[Bidwell: 192]

Soon afterwards, reportedly unhappy with Holkar's leadership, Plumet left his service and returned to the Isle of France. There, only a few years later, Flinders became his neighbour, and an occasional visitor, that officer's estate lying within the six-league radius allowed within the terms of the parole. Holkar was said to have been so incensed by Plumet's desertion that he dismissed all the other Frenchmen in his army branding them as 'Duggerbaz' or 'faithless' [Compton: 580-1].

Flinders' old friends did not desert him, following his decampment from Port Louis. In fact, his removal from the town and from the presence of guards and spies of Decaen, made socializing with the Englishman a more relaxed affair. Writing to John Aken in November 1805, Flinders recorded that Bergeret "has continued to be friendly to me nearly as before, though I think not quite so anxiously". On several occasions

Flinders also sought permission to return to Port Louis, in order to meet acquaintances such as Augustin Baudin who was revisiting the island. On one such visit to town, in May 1806, he breakfasted with Major d'Unienville, the officer who had accommodated him on his first arrival. He informed Flinders that the pilot who had escorted the *Cumberland* to the port had been dismissed from his post [for failing to obey instructions, having piloted the *Cumberland* himself instead of accompanying her], sent on board the *Atalante* frigate, and from there to the *Psyché*, where he had lost an arm in the action against the *St Fiorenzo*. Flinders wrote "when I heard of the misfortune of this poor fellow, of which I had been an unconscious instrument, it gave me much pain" and arranged for the man to be given 20 dollars as a present. He was also entertained by Captain Bergeret, and met a number of other naval men through him including Messrs Moreau and Cap-Martin who had been on Baudin's expedition, and Mr Genève, who was then a planter residing in Black River.

Among the guests was Charles Baudin, no relation to the Baudin brothers, but another officer from the *Géographe's* voyage of discovery. The two men quickly became friends, and when Flinders returned to Plaines Wilhems, he addressed Charles Baudin a warm letter:

> the esteem I have conceived for you, and the obligations I owe you for your generous exertions to alleviate my misfortunes, make me still regret you will be going to sea in a few days. May your voyage be as agreeable and prosperous as the honour and interest of my country will permit it to be: should the chance of war throw you into the hands of any of my brother officers, I have no doubt that you will meet with that humanity and attention which they very rarely fail to accord to enemies so worthy of their arms as the French; but especially to those who, like you, have laboured in the spirit of philanthropy to obviate or to ameliorate the evils of war to its unfortunate victims.

In June, yet another French officer, who had just arrived from India, sent offers of service to Flinders. Colonel Kerjean brought a letter for Flinders from former English POW, Captain Henry, and supplied him with a bundle of the Madras newspapers. Kerjean had a reputation for liberal treatment of English prisoners as Flinders noted: "this is the gentleman who had obtained for Captain Dansey his permission to go to India, and furnished him with money; and who supplied Captain Loan also with a thousand dollars, for his bills". Kerjean was born on the island and had an estate in Moka.

Meanwhile Bergeret, about to depart for France, "promises to do all in his power there, for me" as Flinders confided in his journal. He addressed the following lines to the Frenchman:

the numerous benefits and kindnesses which, with so much disinterested goodness, you have lavished upon many of my unfortunate countrymen, prisoners like myself, have made you the object of much concern and gratitude to ...the whole English nation ... On your arrival in France then, my dear Sir, forget not that I am here ... A Fleurieu, a Bougainville - can such men be strangers to national honour and humanity? - See these celebrated men, Sir, - explain to them the circumstances of my situation, - tell them the plain tale, and that it is towards them, though so distant, that my looks are directed: your own name will give you an introduction, and the cause you undertake will not disgrace it.

Flinders assured the captain that "the many kindnesses you have conferred upon me and others of my unfortunate countrymen will ever make the name of Bergeret dear to my heart".

Back at 'Le Refuge', in Plaines Wilhems, Flinders attended a function in Tamarin where he was introduced to M. Défait, "once captain of grenadiers in the French army of India at the time of M. de Suffren, and a Chevalier of St Louis". They conversed at length on the subject of the French revolution and the war in India. Flinders was becoming accustomed to socializing with the 'enemy' and finding much common ground despite their nations' mutual animosity. On another occasion, after dining with Défait, Flinders recorded, "ate much, drank more, laughed a great deal, forgot my unfortunate situation". He even presented Colonel Monistrol with "three pairs of small shells which I have chosen out of a few that my servant has by chance preserved of those he picked up on the reef in the South sea where we were shipwrecked".

Charles Baudin returned from time to the time to the island in charge of prize ships captured from the English, and never failed to send word of his arrival to Flinders and to procure for him copies of the published Navy Lists which would enable the Englishman to keep track of his friends and relatives in the service. One of Flinders' letters to Baudin amply conveys the conflicting sentiments that his friendships with men engaged in activities hostile to British interests, evoked:

> *The taking so rich a prize as the Warren Hastings, you will be certain, was no very agreeable intelligence for me, but for your sake I am glad that it rather fell to the lot of the Piémontaise than another: that you yourself have received no wound in the action, gives me more satisfaction than perhaps I ought to feel for an enemy.*

Flinders managed to inject both a sense of humanity and a wry humour into his discussions of the war. In March 1807, learning that the *Semillante*, on which vessel Baudin was then serving, had returned to port, dismasted, Flinders wrote to his friend: "I readily conceive how very disagreeable the accident must have proved to you and your brother officers; infinitely more so, than to the mercantile part of my countrymen in the east".

Meanwhile, Flinders waited eagerly for a letter from Captain Bergeret in France. In January 1807, he confessed to his patron, Sir Joseph Banks, "if the increased lapse of time has diminished my hopes of procuring attention from the French government, the departure of my friend captain Bergeret for Paris, and his promise to exert himself to this end, have kept them from totally vanishing". In June the missive finally arrived, but as Flinders remarked to his brother: "he writes me word that nothing was done, or could be, until the return of the emperor from Warsaw; he indeed consoles me with the hope that a decision would be then made, but this, I believe, proceeded more from his good wishes than his faith".

Disappointed, Flinders did not give up, but once again sought out, among his French friends on the Isle of France, someone who might effectively intercede on his behalf, with the French governor, Decaen. He selected Colonel Kerjean, addressing that officer a long letter in April 1807 in which he asked him to "take the trouble to request an audience of the general for me" and if this should be refused, "to reason with him and answer such objections as the general might make against changing my position. Your character, Sir, and the concern you have been pleased to take in my situation, have directed my eyes towards you". Kerjean did not, however, consider himself to be on good enough terms with Decaen to be a useful intermediary, as he regretfully informed Flinders, offering instead to be of pecuniary assistance to the Englishman. Flinders offered a lyrical appreciation of the colonel's sentiments in his reply: "your generous anxiety to be of service to men in misfortune, I can only compare to an impetuous torrent". Apprised that Kerjean was far from being a member of Decaen's inner circle, Flinders took care not to cause him further difficulties by too openly seeking out his company. Thus, in May 1808, Flinders informed the Colonel by letter:

> I passed two days in the town a short time since, and should have done myself the honour of presenting myself at your house, had not the captain-general caused me to be followed everywhere by an orderly sergeant … I thought it prudent to avoid making visits except where it was known I was more particularly intimate, trusting that my friends would excuse the neglect in favour of the motive.

Of course, Flinders' rapport with some of the former French officers was grounded on their mutual change of fortunes resulting from the vagaries of politics. Thus in August 1807, when Flinders accompanied friends on a visit to Admiral St-Felix, he no doubt saw in the "brave old seaman who by the event of the revolution finds himself deprived of his fortune, save a small habitation upon which he at present resides", something of a kindred spirit. Similarly, when Captain Bergeret confided his disgrace at the hands of his own government – he had written "ma situation est affreuse" – Flinders' reply was characteristically sympathetic:

> *your government will surely one day learn to distinguish and to*
> *reward true merit; but whether in prosperity or misfortune, I beg*
> *you to be assured of my high consideration and esteem, and that*
> *it will be a subject of boast for me to preserve a place in yours.*

In fact, Bergeret was to remain in disgrace until the end of the Empire. However, he was later promoted to Admiral, was made a peer by Louis Philippe in 1841, and died a senator, in 1857.

Augustin Baudin was having difficulties of his own, but when he was wounded in a duel with Barbé de Marbois, Flinders was necessarily circumspect, given that he was a friend of both parties. He later mentioned that the men had quarrelled "about some judicial affair', and that one had been wounded in the thigh and the other in the arm and body. Fortunately both recovered from their injuries.

Charles Baudin was also recuperating at the port, having lost his right arm, and sustained a severe stomach wound during a sea battle with an English frigate. More than 25 Frenchmen from the *Semillante* had been killed and Flinders immediately applied for permission to go to the port to visit his friend. Baudin informed Flinders that the wife of the master of the English vessel *Cecilia*, a Mrs Skeene, had nursed him for 3 days and 3 nights. This was a just reward, since Baudin's own conduct was always praised by his English prisoners. Indeed such examples of reciprocity were crucial to the well-being of those engaged in warfare. Flinders considered, for example, that Edward Pellew's previous conduct to Bergeret was at least partly responsible for that officer's kindness:

> *Captain Bergeret had been taken in the last war in La*
> *Virginie, after a brave defence, by Sir Edward Pellew. The*
> *generous conduct of Sir Edward, operating upon a grateful and*

> *honest heart, produced me a warm friend; and my misfortunes*
> *have brought me others amongst the inhabitants of this island.*

While Baudin was convalescing, and learning to write with his left hand, he addressed his first letter to Flinders in July 1808. The Englishman wrote a moving reply that revealed his sadness at the destructiveness of the war, and his conviction of the more beneficial pursuit of science:

> *How often have I regretted, that you who are so well calculated*
> *to pursue researches that might add to the mass of knowledge*
> *and happiness in the world, should have been drawn by existing*
> *circumstances to quit so truly noble a career, for one which*
> *terminates for the most part in producing misfortune either to*
> *oneself or to others.*

Flinders could not prevail upon Charles Baudin to give up his military career, but when the *Semillante* departed for France towards the end of 1808, the young ensign carried with him a number of letters addressed to French savants, pleading the Englishman's cause.

It is curious to reflect that a man, who, according to Flinders, was "son of a deceased member of the National Institute, who was instrumental in placing Bonaparte at the head of the Government" and who was in consequence "patronised by this chief" should be a designated spokesman of the navigator. But it also made perfect political sense. When Flinders learnt that Baudin had been promoted in France, he confided to his wife: "I conceived much hopes that my memorial, supported by its accompanying letters and the efforts of this and other friends, would procure for me at least an order so positive for my transmission to France, that general Decaen would no longer be able to resist; and that this order would arrive by the first ship".

Instead, as the blockade tightened around the island, Flinders feared that any such command would not be able to reach Decaen. He was nevertheless somewhat mollified to learn, with the arrival of the *Venus* in March 1809, that its commander, Captain Hamelin – who had met Flinders at Port Jackson, when in charge of the *Naturaliste* – along with other officers from that expedition, had "made applications to the marine minister for my liberation; and that the minister had several times answered, that an order had been sent out for that purpose". Hamelin also gave Flinders the gratifying news that he had been given an 'honourable mention' in the book of Nicolas Baudin's voyage.

Mr Boucherville, described by Flinders as "an old French officer who had served in Canada, and been wounded and made prisoner at the seige of Quebec", also brought some welcome news. While visiting Decaen to secure the release of his son, then a prisoner of the English squadron, he was told by an aide-de-camp that Flinders' name was on a list of those due to be sent away in the cartel. By this stage, however, Flinders was rightly sceptical, and did not allow his hopes to be unduly raised. In the event, it was not until mid 1810 that Flinders was finally allowed to leave the island. In a series of letters written to friends, such as Colonel Kerjean, before leaving, he expressed his thanks for the warmth and kindness with which he had been received.

Following his return to England, Flinders did not entirely lose sight of his friends among the French officers. As war continued for several more years, he was given numerous opportunities to seek to intercede in favour of French military prisoners. His friendship with Charles Baudin also endured, and in the last year of his life, Flinders received an update of that officer's activities:

Vous m'aviez engagé, mon cher ami, lorsque nous étions ensemble à l'Isle de France, à quitter la carrière meurtrière dans laquelle j'étais engagé et à me vouer à des travaux plus pacifiques, et plus intéressants pour le bonheur de l'humanité en général. Je n'ai pas cru devoir alors suivre vos conseils: j'ai pensé que ma malheureuse patrie avait besoin de tous les bras qui pouvaient la servir ... j'ai été assez heureux, pendant trois années d'un service très actif et très perilleux, pour ne jamais perdre un seul des bâtiments confiés à mes soins, et j'en ai été recompensé de la manière la plus satisfaisante pour mon coeur, par les remerciements publics des villes de Genes et de Marseille qui m'ont, chacune, voté une epée d'or.

Baudin asserted his desire to continue "de travailler à me rendre utile à la marine et à mon pays" and mentioned that he hoped to "retablir mon champ que les Cosaques et les Prussiens ont ravagé depuis 6 mois", and even to pay Flinders a visit in England. He eventually retired to Le Havre, but rejoined the navy in 1838. Promoted to Admiral, he died in Paris in 1854.

There was evidently much warmth of feeling and a sense of community of spirit between Charles Baudin and Matthew Flinders, and it was certainly the case that many French officers – such as Bergeret and Kerjean – went out of their way to offer assistance to the English naval captain. Yet, national feeling and cultural pride were not always effectually repressed. Flinders not infrequently makes reference in his journal to heated discussions of politics with his Isle of France friends. In November 1808, for example, after spending the day with Thomi Pitot and Charles Baudin, Flinders wrote:

> *Persecuted a little upon the subject of politics and national character. … After dinner, my two friends returned to town, and I to Vacouas with mixed sensations of anxiety for my poor wounded friend, regret at parting with him, and that I cannot go at the same time, and gratitude for the interest he takes to deliver me from my bondage mixed with some displeasure at his national animosity.*

That a lone Englishman in a Francophone society during the Napoleonic period, should experienced mixed emotions, was perfectly understandable: that Flinders would come to feel as comfortable as he did, during this six and a half year period, was a tribute not only to those individuals in the government and the military who tried to mitigate his hardships, but to the social graces of the island's inhabitants whom he would meet over the course of his forced exile.

The French inhabitants

The closest friendships established by Flinders during the years of his enforced exile were undoubtedly those forged with the chiefly French colonists of his island prison. Despite their nations' enmity, the inhabitants took pains to provide a warm, supportive environment for Flinders. Thus the man who considered friends so important throughout his life, was blessed with many on Mauritius. They did much more than render his stay bearable: by generously admitting the Englishman into their circle, they enabled Flinders to remain productive, to acquire new skills and experiences, and at times, even to wish for nothing better than that his wife could join him in his island retreat. Those of the colonists – such as Bourbon-based Charles Desbassayns - who were overtly sympathetic to the English cause, generally because they disapproved of the ascendancy of Bonaparte, even offered Flinders the opportunity to indulge his patriotic sentiments. With the rest, his relations were remarkably cordial, and provide an illuminating tableau of human friendship in the midst of the vicissitudes and privations of war.

Within a few weeks of Flinders' arrival in the capital, he was contacted by a young French merchant, who was to become his greatest friend, and strongest source of support. Thomi Pitot, born on the island in 1779, of Breton parents, was orphaned at a young age and educated in France, but returned to the Isle of France with his brother Edouard in 1798 and joined the commercial establishment run by their uncle. Both he and his brother had wide-ranging interests and enjoyed the opportunity to interact with cultivated visitors to their island of whatever nationality. In his book, Flinders would later describe Thomi as "the most agreeable, most useful, and at the same time durable" of the friends he made whilst imprisoned in Port Louis.

Pitot wrote to Flinders on 4th February 1804, informing him that he had asked for a permission to visit the Englishman, but this does not seem to have been accorded for some time, as it was not until 10th August that Flinders reported in his journal:

Messrs. Pitot, merchants in the town dined today with our mess. They were very agreeable and have lent us books and music and behaved more liberally than is customary to strangers, but especially to prisoners and Englishmen.

Thomi Pitot

Edouard Pitot

Flinders' surprise at the kind treatment he received was expressed in a letter to his mother, begun at Port Jackson but sent from the Isle of France, in August 1804. He wrote: "the French inhabitants even, of this island … are disposed to be very kind to me. Four or five different people have offered me any money I may want or any service that they can do for me". On the 14th of that month he learnt that several of the town's residents "had taken the trouble to make particular inquiry into my case, and finding that I had done nothing that could authorize the long imprisonment I had suffered here, intended to make an application to the captain-general in my behalf".

Soon Thomi Pitot was assisting Flinders in his relations with Decaen, and he was to benefit greatly from the advice generously offered by Pitot and other colonists. By the end of September, both Thomi and his brother Edouard had become regular visitors, and their gifts of books and newspapers to the English prisoners, said Flinders, had contributed much "to our amusement and happiness in this confinement". Even delicacies from the Pitots' table made their way into the prison: Flinders, on one occasion enjoyed fruit and fish sent by Thomi, and acknowledged that he was already "under many obligations for his great attention and kindness".

The Maison Despeaux, at the port
[as visualized by Geoffrey Ingleton]

If the pleasant socializing sometimes made the prisoners forget their status, an opportunity was not wanting to remind them of it – and to indicate the dangers their visitors ran of falling foul of their government. On 14th October 1804 Captain Bergeret and his friend Mr. Saulnier, "a principal merchant here", according to Flinders, visited the Maison Despeaux. However on that evening, the lax discipline of the prison was called to account by Decaen's officers, and Bergeret, Saulnier and two others, still inside, were sent for "and had something unpleasant said to them for being here after sunset. Some words arose, Saulnier was sent to the guard house, but on the spirited representation of Bergeret, was set at liberty on the responsibility of B. that Saulnier should immediately go up to the captain-general".

The attentions and efforts made by the Pitots became so numerous, that Flinders' journal is full of references to his Mauritian friends. Thomi brought numerous visitors to meet the hapless English captain. On 27th November, Flinders was introduced to Antoine Bayard, President of the local Court of Appeal, and in December to Mr Descroizilles, a merchant, and the man who had leased Flinders' then residence, the Maison Despeaux, to the government. Pitot also continued to lobby for Flinders' liberty and to offer him suggestions as to how to deal with Decaen. On 1st December 1804, for example, he informed Flinders that information received from Captains Linois and Bergeret suggested that the Captain General was now more favourably disposed, and recommended that the Englishman should write to him "in not such a dry style and independent manner you had made before". Pitot added, "remember always that one work not cautious enough is sufficient to prolong very much your misfortune and the concern of your friends".

Pitot was also instrumental in providing Flinders with access to a letter written by Baudin, then in the hands of a colonist, which underscored the kind treatment received by the French explorer when his ships had arrived, in distress, at the English settlement of Port Jackson. Pitot tussled with his patriotic inclinations and his sense of justice, as he frankly admitted to his friend:

I will own it to you it is with some pain I give you such a proof of a disgraceful contrast between your and our governments' behaviour in the same circumstance. My love for my country would have prevented me to leave you get it, if I was not certain that when making use of this epistle it will not be to my countrymen you will attribute your misfortune but only to its real cause.

At this time, it was believed that the letter would prove a powerful means of securing Flinders' liberty and Pitot requested that the identity of the colonist who owned the missive be kept secret: "it would be perhaps a bad thing for this old man to have furnished to you such a terrible weapon against him [Decaen]".

Pitot's magnanimity extended to many other Englishmen besides Flinders. Nor were the Pitots the only colonists to offer a helping hand to English prisoners. To give but a couple of examples noted by Flinders, towards the end of 1804 Lieutenant Wilkinson and another officer obtained permission to go to India, after 10 months on the island, "through the interest of Mons. Saulnier a respectable merchant in the town". Another POW with whom Flinders became friendly - Captain Larkins of the *Warren Hastings* - was lodged by a colonist in Flacq. Flinders remarked that after the *Piémontaise* brought her prize into Grand Port, the prisoners went by foot to Port Louis and en route,

> *were treated kindly by the inhabitants who furnished the officers with horses; particularly at Flacq where Captain Larkins, on account of a wound in his breast, was permitted to remain there in the house of a M. Belzin, one of those men, of whom there are many in this island, who do not consider an Englishman in misfortune to be any longer an enemy.*

In a letter to Larkins, Flinders was equally fulsome in his praise for that officer's host and for the colonists. Stating that he was sure the Captain would receive the "most obliging attentions and kindnesses from all the inhabitants" as he had, he added, "the worthy man with whom, I understand, you have the good fortune to be placed will serve you as a specimen (rather a strong one indeed) of the general good dispositions of the inhabitants". When Larkins was due to depart, he also emphasized the hospitality of the inhabitants: "it will be impossible that the treatment which I have met with on this Island, can ever be effaced from my memory and the name of Belzin must remain indelibly engraven on my remembrance as belonging to a man possessing everything which a man ought to possess".

Not all of the English prisoners found the colonists so welcoming – usually because they themselves were not disposed to mix with Frenchmen. Thus, when Flinders contacted his fellow officer, Captain Woolcombe, the encounter was cool: "he seemed to me under extraordinary apprehensions of the general and afraid to have any communication with me; and surprised at

41

the confidence I appeared to have in my friends who were Frenchmen". Captain Henry Lynne, who had been captured in the same ship, explained that Woolcombe did not consider it good policy to fraternize with the French, and Flinders responded, "I took occasion to inform him of the general benevolence and hospitality of the inhabitants of the Isle of France: if he has not found it to be true, I fear it must be his own fault".

In Mauritius, Flinders was also enabled to rekindle acquaintances made at Port Jackson, prior to his departure from the Continent that was soon to bear the name he had chosen for it. He reported several meetings, at the latter end of 1804, with the owner of the brig *Adele*, Monsieur Coutance, who had lately returned to the island. The Frenchman declared that he had conversed on a number of occasions with Decaen, and had been shown one of Flinders' letters. From the report of the meeting, Flinders deduced: "The general accused me of nothing else than that of being 'trop vif' - I had shewn too much of British independence in refusing to dine with a man who had accused me of being an imposter and who had unjustly made me a prisoner".

By early 1805, Flinders freely admitted that the varied and numerous attentions of Pitot had "done much to keep off the melancholy that in such cases is too apt to get possession of the strongest mind". In his warmest tribute to Thomi Pitot thus far, he noted: "he has proved himself indeed a true friend to humanity". And the time had now come, when Pitot made perhaps his greatest contribution to the welfare of his English friend. In April 1805 Flinders was informed that his application to leave the capital, to reside inland, had been granted. Pitot was asked to choose suitable accommodation, and settled on the house of a widow, Mme d'Arifat, located at Vacoas, on the cooler central plateau of the island in the district of Plaines Wilhems. The d'Arifats' estate would be Flinders' principal place of residence during the remaining years of his stay on the island, and they would become a surrogate family for the lonely

Englishman. Pitot reported that Mr Bayard, among others, had offered to lodge Flinders, but that since he lived in Flacq "I feared his proposition may not have been agreed to because this part is near the sea and has seen some English gentlemen escape to the cruising squadron". Pitot thus settled for 'Le Refuge', the inland, Vacoas estate of Mrs d'Arifat: "I think this same part of the island is better for you than any other because I have there many good friends".

In May, Flinders introduced his wife, through the medium of his letters, to the character and beneficence of Thomi Pitot:

> Once in a week or fortnight, a French gentleman, named Pitot, comes to visit me, and a most kind and intelligent friend he is. I think he feels more for my situation than I do for myself, for takes the shame of its being his country that oppresses me, in addition. He is not the only friend I have here, but is the most constant, and the only one who will run the risk under this arbitrary government of being thought disaffected, by often visiting me. He has written several letters to eminent men in France concerning me.

It would take some time, however, before he could also illustrate for her, through the same means, his blossoming relationship with the d'Arifats, for in August he was still in Port Louis. There he met his future hosts for the first time. Liberated from the Maison Despeaux, Flinders spent a hectic evening of socialising. He was taken to dinner with Pitot's sister and M. Brunet her husband, called upon Captain Bergeret to pay his respects, and was introduced to M. and Mme Saulnier. He then went to a musical party held at the home of M. Froberville, and, finally, was taken to meet Mme d'Arifat. Flinders' first impression was chiefly of her daughters: "who appear to be amiable, and the oldest of which speaks some English". This was Delphine, with whom Flinders was to become particularly close. He played 'bouillote' with the family, which game, he wrote in his journal "seems to be quite the rage in this island". Flinders was being given a whirlwind introduction to Creole social life!

The next day, he dined with the Saulniers, where he "was treated with civility and attention, and offers of service", and called on Mr Chazal, before making the journey to Plaines Wilhems. The d'Arifat family was remaining in town for some time longer, and it was Pitot who took charge of the move, and accompanied Flinders on a tour of the neighbouring plantations. They visited the Couve family, who invited Flinders, as he said,

> to come frequently, every day if I pleased, to dine and sup, and spend the morning or evening, in a neighbourly way, without ceremony; and here again, as often before, I found much embarrassment, from not speaking French.

Fortunately Pitot was on hand to offer the necessary courtesies and Flinders gratefully accepted their hospitality, not least on account of the two young ladies he met there who were musical and with good voices. Through them, following his friend Pitot's return to the port, Flinders was able to make the acquaintance of the Boistels, M. Prideaux, and Martin Moncamp, among other neighbours. His former acquaintance with the Chazals was renewed, and he was introduced to their in-laws, the Chevreau family. On Tuesday 12th November he met for the first time Mme d'Arifat's eldest son, whom he called Labauve, and who was also to become a firm friend, being of a similar age.

Meanwhile Flinders' friends at Port Louis remained on hand. Thomi Pitot visited as often as he could, and in his absence, wrote letters designed to keep his friend's morale high. Flinders now trusted Pitot enough to share his innermost thoughts with the Frenchman, and had obviously discussed plans for escape, for in one letter Pitot made an attempt to dissuade the Englishman from leaving the island precipitately:

> il me parait peu convenable de prendre le parti dont vous me parlez dans votre dernière lettre. Le départ de Mme Flinders aurait peut etre lieu dans le même moment où vous vous eloigneriez de notre colonie et vous devez sentir combien une telle situation serait penible pour vous et pour elle.

Pitot sought to console his friend that the end to hostilities might be in sight: "c'est quelquefois au moment où tout prend l'aspect le plus terrible que la fin des hostilités doit survenir" and to impress upon him the dangers of encouraging his wife to undertake a long voyage which might lead to her captivity in France or one of her colonies, and leave Flinders without the support which she could otherwise give to lobby for his release. He nevertheless provided several letters for her, addressed to his friends in France, which would provide for her welfare, and serve as a means of credit, should the vessel on which she travelled be captured and conducted there. Mme d'Arifat also provided a letter to one of her friends, and the brother-in-law of Mme Brunet, - who resided at La Rochelle - was prevailed upon to supply 300 dollars, in case of necessity.

In early 1806, Captain Bergeret also visited Flinders, and introduced him to Mr Cap-Martin, formerly a lieutenant from *Le Géographe*, part of the Baudin expedition, but who, having married a daughter of a colonist, Mr Perichon - proprietor of a celebrated plantation known as Palma - had settled on the island. They in turn presented him to Mr Mallac, who, with Froberville and Pitot was a member of the Société d'Emulation, and other local literary groups. The company of such men, and the network of neighbours, did much to ease Flinders' worries. On 7 February 1806, he confided to his journal, after dinner with Mr Chevreau and others:

> These little parties I find useful in taking my attention from my imprisonment, and the other circumstances that occasion me uneasiness; especially since I always find myself treated with an attention rather distinguished and at the same time friendly.

A letter to Ann, written in mid 1806, demonstrated how integrated into the island's French society Flinders had become:

> There is more thought of me here, and I think in France, than in England, or even amongst my own relations and friends, thee always, my best beloved, excepted: a prophet is no prophet in his own country. The desire of the family in which I have now lived six months, is not less to oblige and console me with their friendship and kindness, than that of my friend Pitot: judge then my love, if we could not be happy here: there are many good people in the world besides in England.

Flinders was now so at home in the company of his Creole hosts, that he applied to Colonel Monistrol for permission to visit other relatives of his friends, hoping to spend "four days with Mr. Rouillard at Poudre d'Or and four or five with Mr. Ravel at Flacq". Mr Rouillard was married to another of Pitot's sisters, while the Ravel family was related to the d'Arifats.

This idyllic social life was rudely curbed, when permission was denied. Instead, Flinders took the opportunity offered to make a brief visit to the capital, Port Louis, and rode to town with his friends Labauve d'Arifat and Curtat. Once again, numerous offers of hospitality were heaped upon him:

> During this little excursion I received much civility and hospitable attention from Mr. Curtat, who furnished me with a horse, and invited me to accept an apartment in his house during my stay in town; but my friend Tomy Pitot had provided me with three rooms in a pavilion belonging to the house of his brother in law Mr Rouillard. Mr. Pitot took me to sup with his brother in law, Mr. Brunet, where … I was kindly received.

While at the port, Flinders was also visited by Thomas Lavergne, and called upon Mr Chazal. A couple of days after his arrival, he left town to return via the district of Moka, where he dined with Mr Froberville, and called on d'Arifat's aunt, Mme Lachaise.

A few days later, Flinders met another landed proprietor who wiould become a firm friend. Dining with Mr Chevreau on 23rd May 1806, he was introduced to Messrs Lachenardière, St Suzanne, and Desbassayns, noting in his diary only that he "contracted some acquaintance" with the latter. At the end of June 1806, again in Port Louis, Flinders renewed his acquaintance with the Brunets, and there was able to meet Mme Rouillard and three of her children. "Her eldest daughter, Clementine, played prettily upon the pedal harp", Flinders noted, little suspecting that the young lady would within a year be the wife of Edouard Pitot.

Marie F. Pitot   **L'Amitié – the Pitot residence**

Despite these many and agreeable distractions, as the months of his imprisonment dragged on without an end in sight, Flinders succumbed to depression and considered withdrawing completely from the society which had offered him such respite. As he recorded in his journal on 25th September 1806:

> For many days, nay weeks past, I find myself declining into a state of melancholy and weakness of mind which destroys my happiness and renders me unfit for and miserable in society I could not determine to go in to dinner today, and even formed a resolution of retiring into a house of Mr. Perichon's in the neighbourhood, in order to be alone when I found myself so disposed....in the evening I sent an excuse to Mad. D'Arifat for my uncommon absence, to which she answered with her accustomed goodness.

The next day, he wrote a letter to Mme d'Arifat, informing her of his change of plans, but soon afterwards, Elder returned from a trip to Port Louis, "with a packet of letters from England, which afforded me much consolation". Flinders recovered sufficiently to breakfast with his hosts the next day, and "the soothing consolations and reasonings of Madam D. induced me to abandon my ill-omened project". He later "endeavoured by forcing myself into society to re-establish my spirits".

By this time, Flinders' constant interaction with the colonists had made him very aware of their concerns. Thus, when an inhabitant of his acquaintance, M. Deglos, arrived from India, and in order to avoid the British cruisers off the island, ran his ship upon the coast at Tamarin, Flinders offered "to go down to the wreck which is within my limits, if I can serve him at all with my countrymen". Thomi was then visiting the neighbouring French island of Bourbon (present day Réunion), and in his anxiety to see Pitot again, Flinders sincerely hoped that his ship would not fall into the hands of the British.

Anne. L. de Chazal   *T. A. de Chazal*

During Thomi's absence Flinders spent much time with his neighbours, the Chazals. Toussaint Antoine de Chazal was an accomplished artist – indeed it is he who painted one of the few known colour portraits of Flinders – and encouraged his English friend to join him in a project of painting landscapes. Flinders also enjoyed socializing with Chazal's wife, an accomplished musician, and often accompanied the family on trips to their relatives, for example, to the estate of Mesnil, where Mme Chazal's mother resided. Thomi's absence nevertheless left a large void in Flinders' life. Edouard did not write as often as his brother, and despite his best efforts, Flinders felt neglected. He confided to his journal, in December 1806 "there is a weight of sadness at the bottom of my heart, that presses down and enfeebles my mind. Everything with respect to myself is viewed on the darkest side…I now perceive what is meant by the state of a hypochondriac". Flinders made every effort to keep himself busy: on Christmas Day he gave Mr Chazal a sitting for the portrait which was being painted of him, and further sessions followed into January. He also kept up the language classes he shared with the d'Arifat girls, and instituted a class "teaching the first principles of navigation to the two young sons of my hostess, Aristide and Marc".

It was not until May 1807 that Thomi Pitot returned from Bourbon. When he visited Flinders, John Exshaw, an Irishman who had married into the local Kerbalanec family, came with him. Around this time, Flinders also made the acquaintance of Charles Grant, son of the Viscount de Vaux. This young man had been in the English service as a midshipman, but on being brought a prisoner to the Isle of France, had refused to be exchanged, preferring to spend time with relatives on the island.

In July, once again visiting Port Louis, the journal of Flinders provides an indication of his crowded social life. In the space of two days, he went for a walk with Mr Boand, called on Augustin Baudin, the Kerbalanec family, and Mme d'Unienville, drank tea with Mr Chazal, breakfasted with Pitot and dined out. Afterwards, back at Le Refuge in Vacoas, Flinders quarrelled with his erstwhile close friend, Delphine, and found solace in chess lessons with Chazal, and visits to friends including invitations to the estates of Martin Moncamp and Monneron, near Reduit. He described the garden of Minissy, in this district, as "the best planned and the most agreeable in the island. The number of fish ponds, the extensive shaded allies, where the midday sun cannot penetrate, the labyrinth, the prospects, form a delightful retreat". He also dined with the Perichon family at Palma. October 1807 saw Flinders' hopes of leaving aboard a departing cartel once again dashed, and, in a letter to Froberville of Moka, he confided that he had little alternative but to redemand his parole:

The consequence will most probably be that I shall be closely confined and deprived of the society of those friends whose kind attentions have formed almost the only consolation I am capable of receiving here … In all cases, my dear Sir, I beg you to be

assured of the friendship and esteem I entertain for you and your
good family and how sensible I am of the kind interest you have
taken in my situation.

In the event, Flinders did not renounce his parole and was not obliged to withdraw from his friends. As he later told his wife "the earnest remonstrances and persuasions of my friends here prevented it". During the following year he would again contemplate escape – going so far as to write out his farewell notes to Labauve and Thomi, but once more his friends intervened. As he wrote to Ann "my friend Pitot visits me every month, and continues to prove himself the sincere and affectionate friend I have ever found him". It is clear that without the affection and concern exhibited by his close circle of friends, Flinders might have been inveigled into more than one dangerous escapade.

Instead, Flinders continued to investigate more orthodox means of obtaining his freedom. In October 1808 he addressed a letter to Mr. Curtat, requesting him, as a friend of Barbé de Marbois, to publicise his case with the latter's brother, then a Minister in France. Marbois, who resided in the district of Rivière du Rempart, wrote several letters on Flinders' behalf. He did not entirely give up the idea of circumventing authority, however, in his bid to leave the island, and in August 1809, when fellow POW Captain Lynne was due to leave for the Cape, Flinders made plans to communicate with the British squadron. Should Lynne send back any "interesting and confidential" missives, Flinders suggested that Felix Froberville, then a prisoner at the Cape, who could be sworn to secrecy, might be asked to carry them.

Lynne duly reported back that Amiral Bertie did not favour the proposed escape attempt, but Flinders would not have to wait much longer. In March 1810, he confided to Charles Desbassayns, that a promise had been obtained for his departure, and took care to remind his friend that:
if any case should arise wherein I can be useful to you in
England, you will address yourself to me as to a zealous friend;

particularly in the case where you should have a son whom you
wish to have educated in my country; and of whom you may be
assured I shall have the same care as of a child of my own.

Flinders also, at this time, penned a hasty missive to M. Froberville at Moka, wishing the good news to be imparted to their mutual friends and assuring him "of my sincere affection and esteem for you and Madam Froberville: sentiments which I shall ever preserve, together with the gratitude I feel for remembrance of your constant and friendly kindness to me". A similar letter was addressed to André d'Arifat, care of Mr Ravel in Flacq, asking him to pass on the details of his projected departure to the families he knew in the locality, and underscoring the debt Flinders owed to them. Several other letters, including one to the Airolles family were written in the same vein, and to Mr Sauveget of Rivière Lataniers, Flinders expressed the hope that

should you pursue the intention of embarking with your family
for France, and the fate of war should throw you into the hands
of any of my brother officers, the commanders of His Majestys
ships, you may receive from them such treatment as from your
liberal conduct towards me, and the goodness of your own heart,
you are so well entitled.

Similar sentiments were expressed with regard to the Chazal and Chevreau families.

Flinders' last days on the island were to be spent in a flurry of socializing, as he received the heartfelt congratulations of the many colonists who had offered him hospitality during his years of exile in their land. On 1st April 1810, Flinders spent the day at Rivière Lataniers with Messrs Sauveget and Labauve d'Arifat. Returning to Tamarin in the evening, Labauve presented Flinders with "a pretty tric-trac-board, and also with Chess pieces, to amuse me on the passage to India". On 6th April 1810, he wrote: "went out in a great cavalcade of chaises, palanquins and horses to Chimère". This was the residence of the Pitots at Grand River. Many people attended, and, according to Flinders' journal entry:

some appropriate songs were sung, in one of which was a verse complimentary to the English whom friendship had brought there, and a wish that before a year the two nations might be united as we were at that time. It is my friend Thomi who is always the poet of the occasion. Dancing went on till two in the morning when we supped, and the dancing afterwards continued to daylight.

He continued to correspond with Mme d'Arifat from his lodging at the port. The hoped-for return of his journal prior to his departure, did not take place, but his friend consoled him: "il faut faire je crois tous les sacrifices possibles - il faut sortir de cette isle!" On 8th May, Flinders was ordered to embark on the cartel, and made a last round of visits to friends including Kerbalanec, Saulnier, and Robles, bid adieu to Mme. Curtat, and M. Barbé de Marbois, and packed his trunks. His final goodbyes were for the Pitot family.

In a postscript to a letter composed for his friend Charles Desbassayns in Bourbon, Flinders made a curious confession:

Now that I am certain of going, the pleasure I had in contemplating this event in perspective, is vanished. My heart is oppressed at the idea of quitting my friends here, perhaps forever. There is some talk of peace. Should it take place, I shall probably be sent to pursue the investigation of New Holland; and before three years, shall, as I hope, visit the Isle of France. Even during the war, if General DeCaen be gone, I propose to call here if permitted.

Such was his regret at leaving, that Flinders was even considering a return to the island if it remained in French hands!

In June the *Harriet* sailed, from where Flinders transferred to the *Otter* bound for the Cape of Good Hope. From there Flinders addressed a letter to Mme d'Arifat. He had by now been made aware of the impending British attack on the French islands, and saw the prospect of their conquest principally in terms of the reunion of families and friends which peace would bring with it. As he wrote: "ce que me plait le plus, à moi, dans le perspective de l'Anglification des deux isles, est 1) que votre communication avec Mons. et Mad. Desbassayns ne sera plus interrompue par la guerre, et 2) que je reverrai mes chers amis, … avant deux ans, peut-être avec ma femme". He asked her to remember him to his many friends on Mauritius, and speculated that the forthcoming English government of the island might open new opportunities to her children:

> *Ce changement dans l'isle pourrait ouvrir une carrière à mes jeunes amis Aristide et Marc. … Le commerce qui s'ouvrira de suite avec l'Inde &c. employera beaucoup de vaisseaux; sur l'un desquels Aristide, ou son frère, pourrait faire un essai du métier; et si cela lui convienne, alors, à mon arrivée, je lui proposerais un voyage de découverte avec moi; et les isles restant aux Anglais à la paix, la marine royale lui serait ouverte, ou il l'abandonnerait selon les circonstances et son jugement.*

Flinders also wrote to Curtat from Cape Town, on 24 August 1810, having been delayed there for six weeks, waiting for news of the British capture of Bourbon, which had just been received. To Curtat also he promised: "you will hear from me soon after my arrival, and perhaps see me in the Isle of France before two years are over. Be so good as to remember me kindly to Mr. Barbé and all our friends". On the same date he also addressed a letter to M. Sauveget, informing him: "il est possible que l'évenement pret à arriver à votre isle vous donnerez plus d'envie de retourner en France; dans ce cas … je vous renouvelle l'offre de toute mon assistance, soit en Angleterre, soit pour hâter votre passage en France".

No doubt the momentous news from Bourbon had turned Flinders' thoughts to his friends on the island, for on this day, he also penned missives to Thomi Pitot, M. Saulnier and Mme Kerbalanec. Flinders recommended a number of English officers he had met at the Cape to them. A Colonel Butler was mentioned to M. Saulnier, as "un officier distingué et d'un mérite reconnu". In his own way, Flinders was trying to smooth the transition to English rule both for his own friends, and for the officers who had to oversee the change.

Flinders had not long been back in England, before he was receiving old acquaintances from the Isle of France. On 6 March 1811, he was visited by Messrs Dayot and Henry Desbassayns. The latter having arrived from France, hoped to return to Bourbon. Mr Philippe Desbassayns, who was also in London, took it upon himself to seek the recovery of Flinders' journal, carried away by the departing General Decaen. Henry Desbassayns and his wife remained in England for some time, and the families exchanged a number of visits. Flinders also kept in regular touch with Thomi Pitot by letter. By February, news of the conquest of Mauritius had reached England, and he congratulated Pitot "on our becoming countrymen". No letters were received from the Isle of France during that year, and, as Flinders wrote to Mme d'Arifat at its close, "I begin to be impatient to know how the voyage from Bourbon was completed, what favourable changes amongst you have taken place, and what my young friends Aristide and Marc are doing, or propose to do".

It was not until March 1812 that Flinders heard from the d'Arifats, learning of the marriage of Labauve to Delphine Perichon. From further letters received during that year, Flinders learnt that Thomi Pitot had been obliged to go to the Cape, in an attempt to settle a case before the Vice-Admiralty court there, while Philippe Desbassayns, in Paris, was attempting to organize a cartel to go to the Isle of France. This, however, was rejected, and the only means to reach the island continued to be through England or in an American ship. Later in the year, Flinders heard that his friend Charles Desbassayns, having accepted and soon after resigned a post in the temporary British government of his island, now had a son, who had been named Henry Flinders Desbassayns. In May 1812, Flinders, in his turn, was able to report the birth of a daughter, Ann, to his friends.

In June, Panon Desbassayns arrived in England with his wife, and Flinders secured them a house to rent in London Street. Philippe Desbassayns also arrived in London shortly thereafter. In July 1812, Flinders informed Pitot that both the brothers wished to get their "Bourbon affairs settled, and I hope they will succeed: the former with his lady is fixed near us, and has no intention of returning to France; but Philip goes back in a short time". Up to this date, he had still received no letter from Charles Desbassayns, since his departure from Mauritius, and anxiously wrote for news.

Another French visitor was less welcome. Flinders recorded in his journal, on 23rd July, that "Mr. Philip Couve called this evening; having been refused a permission to go out to the Isle of France, he attributed it to something I had written to Mr. Peel. This Mr. Couve is the most ill-mannered, impudent Frenchman with whom I have any acquaintance". Tempers were evidently fraying in the light of the difficulties experienced in communicating with the conquered islands. Nor was their economic situation more comforting. Responding to a letter from Philippe Desbassayns, Flinders reported to him that according to a communication he had received from the Isle of France earlier in the year "the inhabitants are quitting the island very fast". He was pleased, at least, to be able to be of service to Mme Haumont, in Morbihan, France, who requested Flinders to forward her letters to her sister, Mme d'Arifat.

In November 1812, Flinders at last received a letter from Charles Desbassayns, who was contemplating having his son, and Flinders' namesake, educated in England. He also continued to correspond with Labauve d'Arifat, and to discuss the prospects of a small herd of cattle, which his friend had undertaken to rear for him. The hope for a small income from this investment pleased Flinders, who proposed, with his first revenue from the herd, to send Labauve "a mounted pipe, as a testimony of my friendship and an acknowledgment of your kind care of my interests". With Mme d'Arifat, Flinders delighted in exchanging pleasant, gossip-laden letters about their respective families, and particularly, in transmitting details of his little girl. He also gave her news of his servant Elder, about whom she had inquired. Flinders sent his letter with Mme Monneron, who was returning to the island, and recommended his friend to call upon her, as she could provide "much information of the difficulties which creoles experience in getting out; and perhaps upon many other similar subjects which might be useful to some of your friends". He dined with the Monnerons while they were in London, and took them to visit the Royal Observatory.

In early 1813, Flinders' next letter to Mme d'Arifat informed her that M. Sauveget had determined to return to the Isle of France, while Philippe Desbassayns was again in London, on unknown business. His brother Panon and his wife were also still residing in the capital, and met Flinders on a number of occasions during the year. In April, however, he received a letter written by Labauve the previous December, which conveyed the news of his mother's death. Flinders replied:

The shock was to me as if I had lost my own mother, and most sincerely do I sympathise in the affliction of the family; and deep it must be, for the loss of so excellent a parent and member of society. I communicated the event to Mr. and Mrs. Panon Desbassayns who live close by, and they took a sincere part in our regret.

Monsieur Sauveget, in Paris was also given the news of the d'Arifat family from Flinders, who wrote: "jamais, mon cher M. Sauveget, nous ne trouverons une seconde Madame d'Arifat. Elle fut la plus parfaite modèle de tout ce qui est bon et estimable parmi les hommes, et le ciel n'a plus voulu être sans elle". With regard to Sauveget's own affairs, Flinders assured his friend that his request to return to the island would be taken up with the new British Governor, Farquhar. Labauve would be entrusted with the mission: "qui par ses connaissances avec et les honnêtetés faites aux grands, est bien en état de faire la demande avec succès". He also reported Labauve's comment in his letter that "les colons sont plus heureux qu'ils n'ont été depuis bien des années, cependant, les terres sont sans valeur".

In January 1814, Flinders received an unexpected visitor. The son of Etienne Bolger called for advice, and bringing letters. His presence was a surprise, for as Flinders noted: "this is the son of the commandant of La Savanne, to whose misrepresentations I partly attributed my imprisonment in Mauritius". Flinders does not recount how he received the young man, but he no doubt made an effort to be cordial. The remaining days of January were taken up with visits to several government offices, with a view to obtain Sauveget's permission to return to Mauritius, which he finally received, and took to be dispatched by Mr Desbassayns. Midway through the year, he received visits from some of his former acquaintances – including M Le Cornu and John Exshaw, who were returning to Mauritius.

By this stage, Flinders saw few prospects of setting out on another expedition, or of returning to take a post in the Isle of France, as he explained to Labauve: "without recovery from this villainous disorder I shall in fact be fit for nothing". Despite his illness, Flinders continued to act as an intermediary of the d'Arifat news, and evidently still considered himself as one of the family, informing Mme Haumont in May 1814, for example, that he had no information of what had happened to "nos parens et nos propriétés de Languedoc".

Only a short time later, however, Flinders himself was dead, and his wife was addressing a letter to Thomi Pitot, to inform him of her loss:

> *How much will your affectionate heart be grieved, when you shall be acquainted with the mournful intelligence of the death of my dear Husband, which took place on the 19th of July last, after a painful & most distressing illness of five months - I need not attempt to describe to you, who in some measure knew his worth, what my emotions were in being deprived of such a Husband, such an invaluable friend, nor what I now & must ever feel from such a loss … For more than twenty years, He was the Idol of my heart, the centre of my earthly happiness, & altho deprived of his dear society above nine years absence never for one moment weaned my affection.*

Ann asked Pitot to pass on her sad news to Labauve and to Charles Desbassayns. Flinders himself had already prepared a memento for his closest friends in the islands: in his will he bequeathed mourning rings inscribed with the letters MF to Paul Labauve, Thomas Pitot and Charles Desbassayns [Mack: 250].

The correspondence between Ann and the Pitots would continue for many years, as Thomi and then his sons sought to untangle the financial affairs of Flinders in the islands. When Thomi himself died, in 1821, *Le Nouveau Mauricien* reported that his funeral was the best attended since that of Governor Malartic. A letter of condolence from the British Governor to Edouard Pitot indicated that more than one Englishman had cause to admire and respect his qualities: "Je n'ai jamais cessé d'avoir pour M. votre frère une estime et un attachement bin sincères, pénétré que j'étais de ses vertues sociales, de ses talens et de son devouement à la colonie", Farquhar had written.

Others in Flinders' circle of friends were also at the beginning of illustrious careers when he died. Charles Desbassayns, whose family owned the largest landed estates on Bourbon, was quick to grasp the opportunity that sugar production offered. In 1815 he imported pioneering machinery and began to export sugar the same year from his estate at Chaudron, near Saint Denis. [Defos: 148; Toussaint: 159]. Charles, along with his brother Philippe – who forged a separate career in France - are also credited with helping to establish the Catholic clergy on Bourbon [Prudhomme: 49-51].

Toussaint Antoine de Chazal pursued a political career both in the French and British administrations of his island. He was a confidant, in particular, of the first British Governor – Farquhar, and died at the latter's state house of Reduit in 1822. It can truly be said that Flinders counted among his friends a handful of the wealthiest and most influential of the Creole inhabitants.

The 'neutrals'

During the Revolutionary and Napoleonic wars, a number of foreign merchants resided in Port Louis, where good profits were to be made from the buying and selling of goods seized from East India Company ships and brought in by the French privateers. American and Danish ships were particularly active in this region, taking full advantages of the benefits to be gained from their 'neutral' status. They were, in turn, a lifeline to the Isle of France colonists, whose communication with their metropolis was severely disrupted by the political and bellicose effects of the Revolution. Neutral ships became the chief purveyors of world news, and were regularly pumped for information as to the movements and actions of both sides in the wars that afflicted England and France during this period.

Between 1803 and 1810, when Flinders was incarcerated on the island, 167 prizes were brought in by the privateers, giving foreign traders ample goods to buy, while their own cargoes were snapped up by colonists cut off by the British blockade from their supply ships. While business was brisk, politics did not always favour the Americans: conversely when relations deteriorated with the French government, this adversely affected their compatriots in the overseas territories. In 1803 and 1807, for example, Decaen confiscated two American ships; when he seized 6 more after 1808, commercial relations between the United States and the island ground to a halt, so that in 1809-10, only 11 American ships came into Port Louis, and 6 of these were themselves prizes. [Toussaint, 1954: 2-15]

A number of the foreign residents on the island married into the French community, and became permanent, and well-accepted members of colonial society. This did not necessarily imply that they supported Napoleon or his envoy, Decaen, and indeed several of the foreign 'neutrals' were, as Flinders and his fellow prisoners-of-war discovered, decidedly pro-British in their political sympathies. Such men actively sought out the English officers and not only socialised with them, but undertook potentially risky errands on their behalf.

Within a couple of days of his arrival on the island, Flinders learnt that two American ships, the *Hunter* and the *Fanny* which he had encountered earlier at Timor and Port Jackson respectively, were in the port. Officers of both vessels were among his first visitors at the Café Marengo, on 20 December 1803. Still imagining that he would be set at liberty within days, Flinders proposed to take passage with them to St Helena. On 31st December, however, Flinders learnt that the Commander of the *Fanny* had been questioned as to his visit, and warned not to take letters for him. This was one of the first indications that his release was to be no straightforward matter. Many of his fellow prisoners, however, were able to depart on American ships, which thus constituted a welcome lifeline for English POWs.

The motives of the captains, it should be noted, were as likely to be financial as humanitarian. When one POW, Webb, left the island, on board the *Bellisarius* bound for Salem, Flinders observed that he paid the high price of 200 dollars for his passage. On the other hand, when the *James* departed for New York in May 1805 with a handful of English prisoners, Flinders reported that "the owner Mr Ogden and the captain Campbell have given passages to [them] without any other charge than that of laying in something towards the mess table".

Flinders also remarked in his journal, that he had been visited by "one Dutch, one Swiss, and one Norwegian gentleman ... but not one Englishman although there are many here who are at liberty to walk about". On 11th January, "a benevolent old Swiss", helped Flinders to exchange some of his bills on favourable terms, and continued to visit him regularly. This was probably Johann Boand, whose devotion astounded the navigator. In April 1806 the elderly Swiss merchant made a notable journey just to bring Flinders a copy of the *Times*, which contained a reference to him. Flinders commented: "this old gentleman is not less than 50 years old, yet he arrived on foot here, at seven in the morning and at 4 in the afternoon he set off to return in the same way, refusing to accept a bed here".

By this time, Flinders, now residing in Plaines Wilhems, was well entrenched in local Creole society, and had already observed the important role of the neutrals – particularly the Americans on the island as purveyors of world news, and as propagandists in their own right. In October 1806, a letter from Pitot detailed "all the principal intelligence which had been spread in the town from the American brig which came from London and which seemed to have been rendered palatable to the French taste, according to the American custom". And when another American ship arrived in March 1808, Flinders commented "the last American brings various news, which have the appearance of having been melted down and remanufactured here". In April he explained why the Americans might wish to dramatize events. Noting that an American brig had arrived, bearing the information an embargo had been placed upon all English ships in their ports, and that war between the two nations appeared inevitable, he added: "the American news seems to have been exaggerated for the purpose of selling his cargo".

In November, with British ships blockading the island, Flinders noted another important role of the Americans at this difficult time:

All communication from without being at present cut off by our cruisers ... it is remarkable, that most foreign articles are in great abundance in the town, and as cheap as in time of peace. This the French owe entirely to the Americans who keep them well supplied with articles from France, England and America; but they bring neither rice nor maize, which form the subsistence of the greater part of the inhabitants.

When the Americans did not come to the island, the availability of consumer items fell, and prices soared. In February 1808 Flinders remarked that few of their ships had visited the Isle of France during the preceding year: "in consequence, all articles of importation have long been exceedingly dear". The uncertainty of America's position, together with the cessation of Indian commerce, reported Flinders in May,

> have done much mischief to commerce here, and every article of European or Indian manufacture, particularly the former, is at an excessive price … I gave the other day 20 dollars for a hat that, when I left England, would have cost me 18 shillings… Fortunately for the inhabitants the provisions of the island are abundant and cheap.

On one occasion when Flinders accepted a habitual invitation to dine with his neighbours, the Chazals, he was introduced to an American, Mr. Bickham. Martin Bickham had first come to the Isle of France in 1798, as supercargo aboard the *Sally*, a brig owned by French-American merchant Stephen Girard, who at that time, was seeking new markets for his goods. Bickham's connection with Girard stemmed from his sister Sally's relationship with the merchant. Having no children of his own, Girard took an interest in the Quaker boy from New Jersey - who moved into Girard's home as an 8 year old - and trained Martin as his factor and agent. Bickham found life on the Isle of France conducive, and encouraged his patron to settle him there:

> The situation of this Island is so convenient for trade, and its port so commodious that there will be doubtless a great deal of good business done here. It can be looked upon in a manner, as the Store house of the Eastern world; there are a few places where a more General assortment can be found and it exceeds all places I ever knew for activity in Business; a great deal is done on credit and in exchange of goods for goods; it is a trifling circumstance for a merchant of Reputation to have out Bills to the amount of 150 to 200,000 Dollars. … I propose to you anew to take a Concern with me, at this place and establish a person of confidence, at the principal French settlements in India; by that means two vessels might be constantly employed to great advantage. [McMaster: 353-400]

After their first meeting, whenever Flinders was at the port, he made it a point to meet Bickham.

In May 1806, Flinders made the acquaintance of an American captain, Gamaliel Matthew Ward, commander of the ship *Recovery*. Ward helped to conceive a plan intended to enable Flinders to escape aboard his ship, and although they did not carry it through, when Ward left, Flinders was more than happy to write letters of recommendation for the American. As he wrote to Ward: were the Governor of Bombay, or Admiral Sir Thomas Troubridge, to be "acquainted with the risk you offered to undergo to relieve me from my very extraordinary and unjust imprisonment … your liberal conduct will be duly appreciated by them, and by every naval officer in His Majesty's service".

The 'Good Friends', a ship from Girard's fleet
which visited the Isle of France

There is no doubt that Flinders felt an affinity for the English-speaking Americans, whose dealings with the French authorities on the island were occasionally as misconceived as his own initial contact with Decaen and that general's subordinates. Thus, in his book, Flinders recounted with some humour the misadventure of a "blunt American" sea captain, who "having left a part of his people to collect seal-skins upon the Island Tristan-d'Acunha, had come in for provisions, and to get his vessel repaired. This honest man did not wish to tell where he was collecting his cargo, nor did he understand all the ceremony he was required to go through". The dialogue between the blustering old seaman and the French officer of the port, must have recalled to Flinders his own stumbling attempts to communicate with the captain general's men on his first arrival at the island.

With the assistance of Bickham, who arranged matters with the captains, Flinders also made use of the American ships to forward his letters. In April 1806 Flinders was considering asking his wife to make the journey to the Isle of France to share his exile. His contacts with the American traders on the island gave him the confidence to suggest that she sail via America, where she could obtain letters of credit from Buchanan of Baltimore or Stephen Girard of Philadelphia. Bickham was the agent of Girard, and no doubt recommended his patron and employer to Flinders. And when his servant, Elder, needed to be found a speedy passage home, it was to Bickham that Flinders turned, to find out if any ship was due to sail to America. Elder was duly placed on board the *Phoebe*, bound for Baltimore.

There were plenty of opportunities to socialize with Martin Bickham, who was married to a daughter of Mme Airolles. He was consequently a relative of Mme Chazal and Mme Chevreau – his wife's sisters, and thus frequented the elite social circle into which Flinders had also gained access. On one occasion Flinders accompanied the Bickhams and the Chevreaux on a visit to Mesnil. A second American commercial agent on the island – John Higginson Cabot – was also present at some of these gatherings.

Flinders regularly sought out individuals who could intercede for him with the local or home government, and in April 1807, he wrote to Beckmann, a Danish merchant, who had a reputation for helping to obtain the liberation of English prisoners, to this effect. Beckmann duly visited Governor Decaen on Flinders' behalf, to solicit an audience for the navigator, but returned empty-handed. The Dane was also an acquaintance of Rear Admiral Sir Edward Pellew, then commanding officer of the India fleet, and obligingly carried a letter from Flinders to him.

The 'neutrals' residing at the port were certainly prepared to take risks for their English friends. Flinders informed Admiral Pellew that his Swiss friend Boand was "an upright and honest man" and confided: "I have agreed with him upon a channel of correspondence by which he will transmit to me any letters that you Sir Edward, or any other person may chuse to favour me with, without the necessity of their passing through the hands of this government". In return, Flinders provided Boand with letters of introduction to his friends in India – W H Robertson, a surgeon and former POW, the Calcutta-based merchant John Campbell, and James Franklin, serving in a cavalry regiment. He even recommended the Swiss merchant to his friend, botanist Christopher Smith, believed to be residing at Pulo Penang:

> He is a worthy, good, and strictly honest man: the outside is a little rough, but the interior man is sterling, and he is a staunch friend to the British cause; by the bye, his attachment to England has brought him into many little troubles here, and made him enemies, but he cannot be the less liked on this account by a British subject.

The nature of the risk that Boand took was forcibly illustrated, when his baggage was seized on the eve of his departure. Flinders heard of the incident, and immediately wrote to Boand:

> Be in no apprehension for the consequences to me: there is nothing in them that can with justice be construed to my disadvantage. I am principally sorry that you have lost the letters that were intended for your service...I have applied for a permission to go to town, intending to learn if possible, something from Mr. Monistrol, concerning the scandalous transaction of seizing my letters, and the intentions of the government with respect to me; but as yet I have received no answer ... I beg you either to see, or write to Sir Edward Pellew and inform him of the seizure of my letters.

Flinders later described the incident in a letter to his friend, Major Henry: "The evening before the ship (the *Waldemar*) was to sail, officers of the police were sent on board to search Mr. Boand's trunk, and my letter to you, with many others, were seized". He was not to be made aware for some time to come that Boand had in fact carefully separated the Englishman's letters from his baggage, and had thus managed successfully to smuggle them off the island.

Flinders now had an extensive network of contacts who could be relied upon to exercise circumspection in the transmission of his letters to and from the Isle of France. For example, while Boand was still in India, he asked him to pass on any correspondence for him, to Mr Gourel de St Pern, agent aboard a cartel transporting prisoners there, and when Bickham returned to America in 1808, he was also entrusted with correspondence. Towards the end of his exile, a letter of Flinders to his wife underscored the personal dismay that any interruption to American trade caused him:

> *To increase the distress of my situation, the numerous American vessels that lately visited this island, and by which I was accustomed to write and sometimes to receive letters from England, have now almost totally ceased their voyages, and I fear have cut off the last of my resources to obtain liberty.*

Flinders seems to have lost touch with most of these individuals from 'neutral' countries who were so helpful to him at the Isle of France, but in 1812, when Martin Bickham passed through London on his way to Mauritius, he paid Flinders a visit, and performed one last transit of correspondence for him. After Flinders' death, Bickham became American consul on the island, a post he held for a number of years. His descendants, however, settled in America and France.

PART TWO

Occupations
and
Distractions

*"Mankind are not yet so debased, as to see an innocent man
suffering without feeling an interest for him".*
Matthew Flinders to his mother, December 1806

Les Trois Mamelles

In front of the 'Trois Mamelles' is a steep gap through which the river rushes to the low land of the Tamarin; and there the eye quits it to survey the sugar plantations, but soon it passes on to the Baye of Tamarin, to the breakers on the coral reefs which skirt the shore, and to the sea expanded out to a very distant horizon. When the sun sets in front of the gap, and the vessels are seen passing before it along the coast, nothing seems wanting to complete this romantic prospect.

Matthew Flinders, *A Voyage to Terra Australis*, p 426-27

Scientific Study and Intellectual Pursuits

I ntellectual stimulation was very important to Flinders, and he was gratified to gain admission to a circle of cultivated men and women on Mauritius. Interaction with them facilitated and encouraged the scientific work in which Flinders was himself occupied, almost from the moment of his arrival. And when he was not engaged in chart-making and writing up his narrative, he benefited much from discussions with his acquaintances on the island. He was initially drawn to Thomi Pitot because, as he wrote, "he speaks some English and is very conversant with English books, and celebrated men", and enjoyed the company of Charles Desbassayns, with whom he could have "much conversation upon science and scientific men".

While still at the Café Marengo Flinders busied himself with chart-making: his charts of the Gulph of Carpentaria, and Torres Strait were drawn up at this period. His companions were inevitably also involved in his work: while he wrote up his Admiralty log book, for example, Aken was employed in copying the bearing book and Elder in rewriting the log that was water-damaged during the shipwreck of the *Porpoise*.

In early June 1804, Flinders' incarceration was enlivened by the visit of two naval officers, one of whom, M. Quenot, (Flinders initially spelt the name Canot) was an expert in astronomy: "we had much conversation upon the subject of astronomy and other topics allied to it" recorded Flinders. Quenot later provided him with details of studies of longitude made at the port, which he was pleased to note accorded well with his own calculations, and Flinders delightedly accepted his offer of "geographical or astronomical communications … relative to Madagascar and the Mozambique Channel" to assist him in the construction of his chart of Madagascar. Flinders was also provided with examples of the work of noted cartographer, Lislet Geffroy, and made use of it in his own mapping studies.

Even when he left the port capital to take up residence at the isolated estate of the d'Arifats – Le Refuge – Flinders was far from starved of intellectual companionship. He had been fortunate in Pitot's benevolence, for the latter was a member of the island's literary and scientific societies and was able to introduce Flinders to some of the finest minds of the colony. Soon the Englishman was referring to his "literary friends Pitot, Froberville and Baudin" and describing Thomi as "a young man of considerable abilities and a most excellent heart". Froberville was an author in his own right, and Charles Baudin was one of a number of educated young men who had been part of the rival French expedition to Australia, and whose presence on the island helped to make Flinders' time there an intellectually stimulating one.

Froberville and the Pitots were also members of the Société d'Emulation, a group formed by the artists and scientists who had disembarked from Baudin's expedition. This distinguished group was presided over by M. Foisy, and addressed a letter to the Institut de France, in April 1806, in favour of Flinders. The latter responded in an equally high-flown style:

> The Society of Emulation, has ever possessed my respect and best wishes, as it must of all men who desire to see depôts of knowledge multiplied upon the earth, and the spirit of universal philanthropy extend itself among men, for it is a truth, of which if any are unconvinced, your present generous proceeding must tend to their conviction, that the friends of science are ever the friends of humanity…. your liberal sentiments, your generous exertions, will ever be for me a theme of praise and admiration in whatever part of the earth my labours may call, or my misfortunes may throw me.

Pitot, indeed, was instrumental in securing the interest of French intellectuals, in Flinders' predicament. He addressed letters to the explorer Louis Antoine de Bougainville, the astronmer Joseph Jerome de Lalande, and to other savants. Pitot's letter to Bougainville was a masterful piece of writing, and one that Flinders proudly copied into the narrative he sent to the British Admiralty Office. Pitot had written:

> *Ce n'est pas pour un Anglais, Monsieur, que je vous implore:*
> *en devenant le chef d'une expédition de découvertes, M Flinders*
> *est devenu l'homme de toutes les nations policées, toutes l'ont*
> *adopté, toutes ont vu, toutes ont du voir en lui un ami dévoué au*
> *bonheur à l'utilité générale.*

One of Flinder's biographers has commented that Pitot's correspondents were "all members of the Institut de France, and their support when the Flinders' case was discussed, may have been secured by Pitot" [Ingleton: 320].

De Bougainville   *La Pérouse*

In acknowledgement of the kindness of the Société d'Emulation to him Flinders composed a ten-page mémoire for the Society, "describing Wreck Reef, and giving my opinion upon the loss of the much regretted La Pérouse". The celebrated French explorer

71

was dear to the hearts of educated Mauritians because he had become – briefly – one of their own, settling on the island where he purchased a small estate. In March 1806, Flinders visited the habitation – which happened to be on Mr Airolles' property - that had once belonged to La Pérouse:

> *I surveyed this spot with a mixture of pleasure and melancholy. How happy he had once been in this little spot with his family, and what a miserable fate terminated his existence. This was the spot where the man lamented by the good and well-informed of all nations, the man whom science illumined, and humanity, joined to an honest ambition, conducted to the haunts of the remotest savages; - in this spot he once dwelt unknown to the great world, but happy. When he became great and celebrated, he ceased to exist.*

Flinders prevailed upon Mr Airolles to create an engraved monument to La Pérouse there.

Flinders himself also wrote to eminent French geographer, the Comte de Fleurieu, and other savants in France, as did Amiral Linois on his behalf. As Flinders informed his patron, Sir Joseph Banks, such endeavours were made in the hope "that in time something may be done this way should earlier methods fail".

The efforts made by his literary friends to appeal to the savants of France, was one of the avenues through which Flinders' impatience for liberty was assuaged. Another was through work. In a letter to his brother, along with which he sent his chart of New Holland, Flinders stated that "what with reading, writing and chart making, I am almost as busy in this prison as ever you knew me". Work was a successful antidote to the torment of imprisonment, and almost a way to get back at his captors, he suggested: "their rage is disarmed of its sting, for they cannot make me very unhappy whilst I have useful employment". By November 1805 he had taken his account of the voyage as far as he could with the materials at his disposal, and had begun learning French: "this has been both my business and amusement". His teachers were the young d'Arifat ladies, and his progress was exemplified by the letters he was soon able to write, in French, to Pitot.

His need to keep busy was dramatically expressed in a letter to his friend, Major Henry:

> *the best years of my life are passing away in inactivity; the time wherein I ought to make myself a name is gliding by, unemployed, never to return. When I say unemployed, you who know my restlessness, will understand it within certain limits, for I have always something to do, either in gaining information or with the accounts of my voyage. At present I am occupied in writing a narrative of my shipwreck, with an abridged statement of the circumstances preceding it and a detail of my voyage here and subsequent imprisonment.*

The narrative, of several hundred pages, was completed in 1806 and given to Captain Larkins of the *Warren Hastings* for transmission to Mr Marsden of the Admiralty Office.

A few months later, Flinders was pleased to learn that the charts which Aken had carried with him, had safely arrived in England, and in a letter to Sir Joseph Banks, he hoped that they would afford pleasure to the naval hydrographer, Alexandrer Dalrymple, "and all those interested in the progress of discovery". He was also informed that a paper he had forwarded to his patron "upon the changes that take place in the variations of the compass observed on ship board", had been read before the Royal Society and published in their transactions. Furthermore, as he confided to Pitot, his work had been described in the *Monthly Magazine* of January 1806 "as an ingenious paper". Since its despatch, he had "much extended my observations on that subject". It was certainly evident that Flinders was not idling away his years in captivity.

Flinders also wrote to the Governor of Port Jackson, "giving him a comparison between my observations and his in Torres' Strait, and enclosing a paper, which described the manner of preparing maize for the table in the Isle of France". Flinders considered that the method of rendering this easily grown vegetable palatable would be useful to the colonists of the small British settlement, who often suffered food shortages, and had made extensive notes on the subject:

The manner of treating the maize in this island seems to me ingenious. It is ground between two stones after the ancient manner and afterwards sifted thus. A flat basket in the shape of a large round dish, made of the filaments of vacouas, is used ... by a movement from N.E. to S.W. and a cant of the basket after each double movement, the yellow maize is then separated from the fine white flour, which being more tenacious, remains at the bottom of the basket: the maize is thrown out upon one piece of cloth and the fine flour put into a sack, being done with. The maize is then taken into the basket again, deprived of the husks and fine flour, and by a movement backwards and forwards, the coarse maize is made to come to the nearer part of the basket, and the finer to the further part: as they separate they are taken out and put upon different cloths .... The finer maize is put on one side, and the coarse on the other. The husks are food for the hogs, the bran boiled with water for the ducks, the coarsest maize for the fowls, the white flour is sometimes made into cakes with sugar, but is more commonly boiled up for the dogs, and it is the finer yellow maize only which is boiled, and served up dry, like rice, upon the table of the planter.

In a letter to Charles Grimes, Surveyor General in New South Wales, Flinders added "if you can overcome your prejudices, you will find it an excellent substitute for rice and even for bread, in the country or in case of necessity: the greater part of the farmers in this country make use of little else". Flinders also gave a good account to Grimes of his scientific pursuits:

although in confinement, three-years and a half, have not wholly passed in doing nothing. I have nearly completed my charts, written much relating to the Investigator voyage, made myself master of the French Language so far as to write and speak it intelligibly, and have recalled to my recollection many subjects of my early studies; besides having gained, I hope, much useful experience, and several valuable friends.

The 'several valuable friends' no doubt referred to the many French inhabitants Flinders met, who had themselves travelled widely and read much, sharing their views and experiences with him. In October 1805, for example, on a return visit to the port, he made the acquaintance of M. Murat, who had taken part in the celebrated voyage of M. Etienne Marchand, the account of which, by Fleurieu, Flinders had read. They conversed "upon nautical subjects", and the Englishman found him "well informed". Later, Flinders borrowed le Marchand's five volumes, from M. Cazeaux, the civil commissary of Plaines Wilhems. They gave him further insights for his work on magnetism, which was also materially assisted by his friend Charles Desbassayns, who addressed him a long letter, "from which I learn that Humbolt and Biott had made researches into the magnetism of the earth similar to those which occupy me at present". Charles also gave Flinders a copy of *Le Traité élémentaire de Physique* and a letter of introduction to the French chemist, Vauquelin "in case I might be sent to France". When Desbassayns asked his opinion of the treatise, Flinders judged it "excellent" but drew attention to errors in the work. He also informed his friend that he had been pursuing his studies in trigonometry, "which are founded our operations at sea for finding the latitude, longitude etc".

Flinders sent regular reports of his studies to his patrons and superiors in England. Describing his researches "on the magnetism of ships, and on the effect of sea and land winds upon the barometer", to Sir Joseph Banks in September 1808, Flinders frankly avowed,

> Since I have no longer had anything to occupy me relating to the Investigators' voyage and found myself sufficiently master of the French language, I have endeavoured by such researches to employ my time usefully to the public and to myself. I do not pretend to claim any merit from this, for to employ myself constantly is a necessary consequence of the habits I have contracted, and is the only means I have to prevent my mind from dwelling too intensely upon the circumstances of my imprisonment and the losses in every way that I sustain from it.

To Alexander Dalrymple, Flinders described the chart of the coast of Australia which he had sent home from the Isle of France, informing him: "I regret much that the decayed state of the Investigator did not permit me to make a thorough survey of Torres Strait. In default of that, I have combined the different authorities with which you furnished me, with my own observations there, and trust the result is a valuable chart".

Alexander Dalrymple

Sir Joseph Banks

Constantly searching for gainful employment, on one occasion he borrowed a compass from Chazal, intending to verify extant charts of the Isle of France by taking bearings of the area within which he was given access according to the terms of his parole. Fortunately he was not short of useful distractions. On a visit to Tamarin, he made the acquaintance of Laurent Barbé, son in law of the celebrated Céré, then superintendant of the botanical garden on the island. His relative informed Flinders that Céré "had a regular meteorological journal kept during 50 years in this island" and was writing an account of the local flora.

Flinders used his newly acquired knowledge of French to familiarize himself with travel accounts in that language and other scientific treatises. His reading material while on the island included five volumes of Le Vaillant's travels in southern Africa, which had been presented to him by Charles Desbassayns. Flinders also found time to read and comment on Barthelemy de Froberville's pioneering French novel, *Sidner or the Dangers of the Imagination*. Evidently, his distinguished friend had requested Flinders opinion on his book, which was given in July 1806:

> *The events seemed to me to be conducted with much simplicity, and agreeable to nature. ...Upon the whole, benevolence, active charity, and the necessity of moderating our passions, in order to be happy, are inculcated throughout, and the author undoubtedly merits the praise of society for his work ... accept my thanks for the pleasure and instruction which your little book has furnished.*

Barthelemy de Froberville

Late the following year, two days were set aside for a visit to the Moka home of M. de Froberville, who was then editing a voluminous Madagascan travel account:

> *Mr F. communicated to me a manuscript history of a Madagascar chief, named Ratsimala-o, celebrated for his bravery and humanity. Mr F. had composed this history from the notes of Monsieur Mayeur who had passed 30 years in Madagascar, travelled over most parts of it, and had been intimately acquainted with the son of the chief.*

According to Flinders, Froberville sought his assistance for the publication of this manuscript, giving him authority either to take the material to his brother in France, or to translate and publish it in England. Flinders added "these labours have occupied M. de Froberville during two or three years, but at present his health, and particularly his eyes are so deranged, that he finds himself totally incapable to prosecute it; and from the circumstances of the war, from making public what he has done". Ultimately, however, Flinders returned the materials to Mr Froberville before his departure from the island.

Flinders' interest in his island surroundings extended to the study of local pursuits such as the manufacture of indigo, - he provided detailed descriptions in his journal of the techniques he witnessed, and even tried out for himself. He also sought to understand the geological history and volcanic origins of the Isle of France, and made many observations from his excursions around the island. Desbassayns brought him a specimen from a limestone mine of a fellow colonist and Flinders considered it to "have been formed by the deposition of calcarious matter from either the sea or a spring in the hollows left by the volcanic lava; some pieces of the common stone are mixed with it, being probably rolled down by the torrent or sea". Desbassayns and another friend had opposing views as to the original formation of the islands, and Flinders enjoyed listening to their discussion, which he said, confirmed his opinion "as to the former existence of volcanoes in the island, and that the stone is, with very rare exceptions, a lava which has been more or less fused".

Despite these activities, the realisation, in 1809, that while he was kept incarcerated, his discoveries had been usurped by his French rivals, was a bitter pill for Flinders to swallow. As he told his wife: "the before unknown part of the south coast of Australia was principally discovered by me; but at Paris they have given it the name of Terre Napoleon, two gulphs of my discovery are called Golphe Bonaparte and Golphe Joséphine, my Kangaroo Island is changed into l'Isle Decrés". To Sir Joseph Banks, Flinders complained, "whilst general Decaen keeps me a prisoner here, they search at Paris to deprive me of the little honour with the scientific world, which my labours might have procured me". He even speculated that his continued imprisonment was related to what he termed "this invasion of the maritime reputation of England". In a letter to Charles Desbassayns, Flinders contrived to convey more cheerful news – he had been informed by Captain Hamelin, that the publication of Baudin's voyage made honourable mention of him, and that all of the officers of the *Géographe* and the *Naturaliste* had joined in their endeavours to secure his liberation, while in the work itself, justice had been rendered to him in the demarcation of the discoveries of the two explorers.

Fortunately, the time was drawing near when Flinders would himself be back in England and at liberty to complete his book of the Investigator's voyage. And it proved an arduous task: in August 1811, from London, he informed his friend Pitot: "I am so pressed on all sides to get the voyage published quickly, that every instant is devoted to it, except the time that is required by indispensable business". Unfortunately Flinders' journal remained in the hands of General Decaen – who was rumoured to be keeping it, "for his own justification". In March 1812, the journal was still with the French general, although by this stage, Philippe Desbassayns and both governments had become involved in the struggle to wrest it from that officer's grasp.

Before completing his book, Flinders undertook a few more experiments on magnetism. In July 1812, he requested and secured the Admiralty's support for a trip to Portsmouth, "to make experiments upon the errors produced in the compass by the attraction of ships". Flinders was pleased with the results, and hoped, through them

> to obviate the errors, and prevent the recurrence of those losses of ships which have arisen from allowing a wrong variation to the compass. Should the Admiralty adopt the plans I have recommended, navigation and hydrography will receive a greater degree of advancement towards perfection than they have done for many years.

79

Flinders' contribution to work in this field was to discern the pattern, - and its nature and extent – of the observed differences in compass bearings which had frequently been noted: "slowly but surely Flinders' correction for the vertical component in the earth's magnetic field became standard equipment on all ships throughout the world". [Mack: 223].

Back in London, Flinders returned to his work on the voyage, and was informed, again through the medium of Philip Desbassayns in Paris, "that Baudin's voyage is not yet finished. Peron's second volume is in slow progress, and the nautical part, with the charts, are in hand; but when they will be published seems quite uncertain". Having himself read the first volume of Peron's account, Flinders found that the story of "the encroachments upon my discoveries was correct". In a letter to Philippe's brother, Charles Desbassayns of Bourbon, he even speculated that Peron was delaying the publication of his chart in order to see those of Flinders first: "after robbing me of the honour of a first discoverer, they may also pilfer me of the details".

By 1812 Flinders had more or less given up the idea of embarking on another voyage, and revisiting the Isle of France en route. As he wrote to Pitot:

There is no talk of prosecuting discovery; and I have no intention of applying for a ship in the common line of service. It is therefore likely that I may retire into Lincolnshire, my native province; to live upon my little income, and divide my time betwixt my garden and my study.

Fortunately Flinders was able to complete his work despite bouts of ill health that would tragically bring about his death, shortly after his life's achievement was printed and placed in his hands. He had received few honours in his lifetime – although he was pleased to be given some recognition by the Natural History Society of Edinburgh, who elected him a member in April 1811 – and indeed for many years after his death, his relatives received almost no recompense for his labours.

Kirstie Archer has summarized the main achievement of Flinders' years of confinement as follows:

> *While waiting for release Flinders set about producing his great map by piecing together a jigsaw puzzle of charts. Until Flinders completed his map the true outline of the continent was not known. The final map was so accurate that it was not superseded until the era of aerial surveys.*

That he achieved so much while at the Isle of France was not only a testimony to Flinders' doggedness, but in no small part due to the moral and material support of the friends he made there. As has justly been argued, "a handful of colonials undertook, despite the risks, to befriend him. They were a small, tightly knit coterie of cultivated people … savants in spirit … it is indeed doubtful whether Matthew Flinders could have survived these years without them" [Mack, p. 202]. On Flinders' last day on the island in May 1810 he was offered a diploma as corresponding member of the Society of Emulation. It was a suitable token of the esteem and friendship that had nourished and inspired Flinders during six and a half long years.

Grand Bassin

Flinders correctly speculated that this upland lake on Mauritius was the crater of an extinct volcano

Port Louis, from the mountain

"how kindly and with what attention I was treated by my friend Pitot as also by Captain Bergeret, and many other French inhabitants, as also by Mr Bickham and Mr Cabot, American merchants and agents. I renewed my acquaintance with Major Dunienville of Savanne who had treated me so politely on first arriving at the island, and also with M. Boand my Swiss friend, whose anxiety to serve me when a prisoner at the Cafe Marengo had not yet lost anything of its ardour".

Extract from Flinders' journal following a visit to Port Louis in 1807

Le Refuge, at Vacoas
[as visualized by Geoffrey Ingleton]

People and Places:
Island Sites and Society

F linders mixed in an elite circle of landed proprietors and merchants – the crème de la crème of Isle of France society - whether composed of old noble families or newly celebrated savants and military men. Many of the families he frequented were wealthy, dividing their time between town houses, and extensive country estates. This was a slave-owning society, and Flinders was necessarily thrust into social situations that were unfamiliar to him. It was also in many ways virgin territory. Settled less than two centuries earlier, despite the many encroachments made on native forest since then, Flinders' years on the island predated the massive clearances which ushered in the island's economic apogee as Britain's premier sugar colony. He was thus able to explore many sites of outstanding natural beauty, of which he took full advantage.

1. The Port Town

During his initial incarceration at the port capital, Flinders' mobility was severely circumscribed and consequently his record of that time chiefly concerns his daily routine within the Maison Despeaux, the garden prison to which he and his companions were moved 4 months after their arrival:

> Before breakfast my time is devoted to the latin language…
> After breakfast I am employed making out a fair copy of the Investigator's log in lieu of my own which was spoiled at the shipwreck. When tired of writing, I apply to music, and when my fingers are tired with the flute, I write again until dinner. After dinner we amuse ourselves with billiards until tea, and afterwards walk in the garden till dusk. From thence till supper I make one at Pleyels quartettes; afterwards walk half an hour and then sleep soundly till daylight when I get up and bathe.

The musical evenings were occasionally enlivened by Pitot and some of his friends, whose accomplishments in this field were greatly appreciated by Flinders. This routine was a dramatic improvement on life in the Café Marengo, where they had been entirely shut up. At the Maison Despeaux, by contrast, he wrote,

> *we have our own apartments and servants, and a garden of about 2 acres in which we walk as we are disposed. ... as prisoners we have little to complain of except that we are not permitted to live at large on our parole or to partake of any amusements beyond our garden wall.*

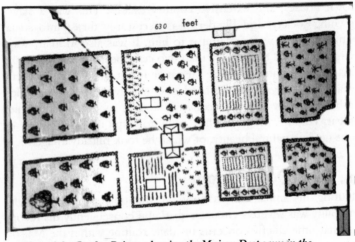

Plan of the Garden Prison, showing the Maison Despeaux in the middle, surrounded by orchards, and guardhouse at bottom right
[*after Ingleton, from an original plan in the Mauritius Archives*]

Even from within the walls of the Garden Prison, however, Flinders' visitors brought tales of their island society that enabled the Englishman to make some comparisons with his own. In October 1804, for example, he remarked:

> *Two gentlemen have been just killed here in duelling, a circumstance that rarely occurs amongst the French. They usually fight with small swords and a scratch or prick usually settles the business; but those confounded English weapons, pistols, are getting into vogue.*

84

He also learnt something of the wider world from those of his fellow prisoners permitted greater latitude than himself. Thus on 16 June 1805 he reported that two of the Englishmen had been given permission to go into town "to be spectators of procession of the hosts and other Catholic ceremonies, this being what these people call 'le fête de Dieu': several salutes were fired today in honour of the fête". On 15th August 1805 he remarked that there were more gun salutes for the celebration of the "fête of the holy virgin" and the church was "ornamented with the flags of all nations".

By July, Flinders was looking forward to obtaining permission, through his friend Captain Bergeret, "to live somewhere in the country, where I can take exercise, and not be shut out from all the world as hitherto I have mostly been". This was granted within the month, and prior to his move Flinders was treated by French officers to an evening at the Port Louis theatre. He understood little of the play, which was in French, but took great notice of the Creole ladies present:

> It surprised me to see so many handsomely dressed women in the pit; the greater part of them must be the wives and daughters of tradesmen, but their dress was, beyond all comparison, more expensive and gay than those of the same class in England.... They seemed to have good clear skins, and well turned necks and bosoms, for the most part; and large eyes that were by no means destitute of power.

This brief exposure to island society led Flinders to make two observations that indicate his essentially reserved nature: he was shocked by the décolleté form of dress adopted by the ladies, and by the "libertine conversation" of the officers who accompanied him home. These would not be the only occasions when Flinders would feel awkward in the company of his less prudish French companions.

On August 20th 1805, Flinders was liberated from the Maison Despeaux but before setting out for his residence in the country, was launched into the town's French society by his friend Thomi

Pitot. Musical parties were organized, and a large gathering assembled at the home of Jacques Deglos, a merchant of the town, and a relation of Pitot. Flinders felt keenly his lack of fluency in French and the novelty of the company of women, and was embarrassed, but grateful for 'French politeness': remarking that despite his awkwardness "no signs of risibility were apparent".

Flinders returned to the port several times, when he gained permission from the authorities to do so. On one occasion, he visited the Champ de Mars, to watch the exercises of the National Guard. On another visit, to purchase gifts for the d'Arifat family, he was entertained by the Pitots and their relatives, the Rouillards and the Brunets.

2. The Country Estate and Environs

Flinders' first excursion following his liberation from the Maison Despeaux in 1805 was to the Pouce mountain. He set off early one morning with Edouard Pitot, Thomi's brother, to make the 3 mile walk from the port, and the men enjoyed wild raspberries as they ascended, and admired the views. However rain set in, and obscured the views, so the outing was cut short.

Prior to leaving the port the Pitots introduced Flinders to his future neighbours in the Vacoas region, then took him to spend a few days at their country house at Grand River, about five miles from town. Here he was initiated into the game of 'bouillote', a common pastime of the colonists, and taken hunting – for hares - with Frederick and Robert Pitot. Later Chazal would also teach Flinders how to play chess and other popular board games.

On the day appointed for the trek to Le Refuge in Vacoas, a picnic lunch was organized in the grounds of Reduit, the governor's country estate, then under renovation, after which the male members of the party continued on to the plantation of Jacques Plumet. Flinders remarked, "he received us with the hospitality, which it seems is not yet vanished from the Isle of France" and enjoyed a walk over part of the 400-acre estate, to see his coffee and clove trees, and a fishpond. The evening was spent at the billiard table.

Flinders paid close attention to the countryside as the group ventured further inland:

> From the time of quitting the port, we had been continually ascending ... and I found a considerable difference in the climate and productions. ... A vast advantage ... is the abundance of never failing streams of water ... We directed our route to the south westward, through intricate paths and crossing different habitations ... sugar, coffee, maize and manioc.

At Le Refuge, Flinders "took possession of two small pavilions, one for myself, the other for my servants". Mme d'Arifat supervised the arrangements from the port, assuring her tenant "je desire beaucoup que vous trouviez dans ma petite solitude quelques commodités et agremens". In his first days there, before the arrival of the d'Arifats, he described his daily routine thus:

> At 6 or 7 o'clock, I rise and walk to the stream behind the house and bathe, and by the time I have shaved and dressed it is eight o'clock, I drink tea and coffee, and eat eggs and bread-and-butter in no small quantity, sometimes with radishes and salad. Afterwards I walk out for two hours, exploring the different roads, streams of water, and plantations in the neighbourhood... At 11 or 12, I sit down to write, or to read French, or to musick, till dinner; I then eat heartily, and afterwards walk out either to make some call or look about till dusk. After tea, musick, reading, and walking before my pavilion occupy my time till eight oclock, when I sit down to supper and soon after go to bed.

Flinders paid several visits to the Chazal's, and was shown around their extensive estate, which he described as being around 1,000 acres in size, its elevated location offering views of the sea and of a waterfall. On 5th September he made an excursion with some neighbours to the Mare aux Vacoas: which he termed, "an irregular piece of water, perhaps a mile long, but in some parts very narrow. ... The lake is surrounded by gently sloping hills, from which there falls, as we were told, seven or eight little streams into the lake". The lake, he was informed, was the source of three rivers – those of Tamarin, Rempart and Papayes, the branches of which "wind round and through the plantations of M. d'Arifat and M. Couve".

A week or so later, Jacques Plumet rode out to Le Refuge, and proposed another trip – to the crater of a volcano (the Trou aux Cerfs), promising also to take him to the residence of Martin Moncamp and to introduce him to another of his neighbours, Mme Airolles. Flinders immediately wrote to Thomi Pitot at the port, requesting him to join the party.

Meanwhile, he made an excursion to the picturesque Tamarin waterfall: walking around and into the bed of the river, below the cascading water. Flinders estimated the cascade to be above 200 feet in height and deemed it a "very beautiful fall of water". Flinders spent two days walking around the falls, and wrote an enthusiastic letter to his friend Pitot urging the brothers to visit, and proclaiming that he was now qualified to be their guide: "it must be seen, and with the mind of a poet or a painter, to be thoroughly understood; the description from a man who is neither, must be very inadequate to give a moderate conception of its grandeur", he told them. When heavy rains increased the volume of water, "the prospect must indeed be grand", he judged. In February 1806, after a prolonged spell of wet weather, Flinders did indeed return to visit the falls:

> Looking down into the abyss of froth and spray was a magnificent sight, for the water in the basin below could not be seen. On stopping my ears with my fingers for a few seconds and withdrawing them suddenly, the noise of the cascade was like the report of a cannon fired close to one, or to a sudden clap of thunder.

"After many incidents of fortune and adventure, I found myself a commander in the Royal Navy, having been charged with an arduous expedition of discovery; have visited a great variety of countries, made three times the tour of the world; find my name known in more kingdoms than that where I was born, with some degree of credit; and this moment a prisoner in a mountainous island in the Indian Ocean, lying under a cascade in a situation very romantic and interior, meditating upon the progress which nature is continually making towards a moderate degree of equality in the physical and moral worlds; and in company with a foreigner, a Frenchman, whom I call, and believe to be, my friend".

Matthew Flinders, at the Tamarin waterfall, October 1805.

Flinders' lifestyle at Le Refuge was far from displeasing to him. In early October 1805, a journal entry stated: "I cannot say that, at present, I am very unhappy. Time has softened my disappointments, I have my books, am making acquisitions in knowledge, enjoy good health, and innocent amusements for which I have still a relish". A few days later his fund of 'amusements' was to be greatly increased by the arrival of Mme d'Arifat accompanied by her teenage daughters, and two young sons. Flinders dined with the family, but refused his hostess' offer to reside with them in the main house. Instead, she pressed Flinders to join their table on a daily basis. Flinders initially refused, but soon found the family's company so agreeable that he reversed his decision, and, insisting on paying a share of expenses, rapidly became a fixture at the house, participating not only in meals but all social events.

In a letter to his brother, Flinders reiterated these happy circumstances of his exile, adding that his health had benefited from the cooler climate of the highlands and that he found "the neighbouring gentry civil and hospitable". Writing to John Aken, Flinders also noted, "the sole restriction upon me is, that I have given my parole not to go beyond six miles from the habitation: this is liberal treatment for a spy".

On 15 October 1805, Flinders embarked on another excursion with Mr Murat, this time to visit Grand Bassin and to climb Le Piton. Flinders noticed a small island in the middle of lake "to which it is said the deer swim off when they are hard chased". After breakfast, the men climbed the Piton hill:

we had a view of the sea for near three-fourths round the compass; the Grand Port, the little islands off it, and the neighbouring parts … From the top of the Piton, I saw that the depth of the basin must be very considerable, and that it descended off from the sides usually in a steep precipice. I have been told by several people that in the deepest part there are more than eighty fathoms in it. It contains eels, some of which are said to be so large as to carry down a deer; and there are

chevrettes, or shrimps of a large size… It appears to me that the
Grand Bassin has been the crater of a volcano.

As Flinders' circle of acquaintances continued to expand so too did the prospect of excursions to their estates and neighbourhoods. On a visit to one property belonging to Mr Curtat, he met Mr Foisy, the President of the Society of Emulation, while another outing to that gentleman's estate in Tamarin, provided an opportunity to explore the seaside, "where the two rivers of Tamarinds and du Rempart throw their waters into the sea" and to visit the sugar and cotton factories of his host. Tamarin became a favourite place of resort for Flinders and his new friends, and many weekend fishing outings were organized. In July 1808 he described a typically convivial day in his journal:

All our company went to the Bay of Tamarinds to fish and
spend the day which we did gaily, having good success with the
seine. Mr. Boucherville, commandant of the quarter, Mr. Cap-
Martin, and M.M. Duguilio joined us at dinner, so that we
made all together about 25 persons. In the evening the ladies
waltzed to my flute and afterwards we played at chess and cards.
M.M. Pitot and Bayard left us after supper.

His increasing familiarity with this part of the island, made Tamarin an obvious choice, when Flinders was laying plans to escape from the island. He spent 4 days cutting a path to the summit of the 'Tourelle', indeed one of his biographers suggests, "it could have been called Flinders' Lookout, from where the desolate navigator searched the horizon for the phantom British men of war sent to rescue him" [Ingleton: 361].

During his years at Le Refuge Flinders, on terms of such intimacy with the landed proprietors, learnt much about their lifestyles and surroundings. He noted that it was customary for the islanders to invite guests to their 'habitations', which word, he explained, meant not simply a dwelling, but referred also to the land the owner possessed. Land concessions given out by the French government were usually 156 French acres in size, so that this became the typical size of a habitation. Flinders also remarked that a habitation would commonly be divided into portions, separated by paths planted on each side

> with rows of vacouas, or planted with the tall jambrosa, to form agreeable shady walks. Behind the rows of vacouas, bananas, pineapples, peach and other fruit trees are planted. Vetiver grass is also planted, cut every year to be used as thatch. Bamboo is planted at the sides of rivers, and gardens enclosed with hedge rows of China rose.

Vacoas, where Flinders now resided, had a cooler, wetter climate than the port, and one advantage he soon found was that "the clouds of mosquitos, black and sand flies, swarms of ants and wasps, the centipedes, scorpions and lizards with which the lower parts of the island are tormented are almost unknown here. Fleas and cockroaches are also less numerous".

Flinders' participation in the social activities of the colonists, also gave him an opportunity to observe the cultural differences between the English and the French. After a hunting trip with the 27 year old Labauve d'Arifat and his friends – La Chaise and Frichot – he noted in his journal: "on comparing the conversation with that of three young Englishman of the same age and class, it appeared that they were more brotherly with each other, more kind in their language, each speaking to the other in the second person singular; but they were more free in their language and ideas also".

Labauve became a freemason while Flinders was living in the family home, and the Englishman recorded the gathering for his initiation, when Messrs Curtat and Pepin attended. The celebration of the fête of St John at the nearby Freemason's lodge was the occasion. Flinders remarked "masonry is much in vogue in this island, there are three lodges in the town, the triple alliance, the peace, and the fifteen artists, and in this quarter the friendly cultivators". Of course, it was not only such masculine activities that Flinders recorded. He participated in many family gatherings and was very comfortable in female company.

3. Morals, Marriages and Miseries

Flinders, indeed, valued friendship very highly, and was overwhelmed by the warmth of Creole society. As he testified: "the friendship, the kindness, the hospitality with which I have been treated during my long detention, by all the inhabitants of this island with whom my circumscribed limits have enabled me to make acquaintance, is beyond all praise". A man who delighted in the company of bright, young women, Flinders was charmed by the d'Arifat girls and their female friends. On an early visit with them to their neighbours, the Couves, he speculated that the daughters of both families would easily cut a swathe in a settlement like Port Jackson: "they would not remain long unmarried; whilst in this island they will scarcely obtain husbands: young women are much more abundant than young men here". On another occasion, dining at Palma with the Perichon family, he records that he spent "an agreeable afternoon with the beautiful ladies of the house".

Flinders particularly enjoyed the company of Mme Chazal, who was "an excellent performer upon the harpsichord" and "one of the most agreeable women I have ever met with". She reportedly possessed a fine English instrument, taken in a prize, and for which she had paid handsomely. Surrounded by female friends, Flinders' confidence and sense of well being became such that he even began to participate in their dance parties. He had the opportunity of seeing what he described as "French contra-danses and waltzes" for the first time at a party held by the Chazals, and on a Saturday in November 1805, even ventured to "waltz for the first time, with my two fair instructresses" at a 'thé dansante' organized by Mme Couve. A few days afterward, he penned a portrait of his new family circle in a letter to his wife. He described Mme d'Arifat as an elderly widow of "excellent understanding and disposition", and added, "it is with the eldest son, of about 27 years, and the eldest daughter of about 20 that I have more particularly attached myself". Evidently, he had talked of Ann to the d'Arifat girls, for he remarked that Delphine was anxious to make her

93

acquaintance. Later he would write to Ann that the girls had woven a necklace of their hair for her. The language classes by now consisted of conversing solely in English on one day, and in French on another: "we even talk upon religion and politics, and though we are almost constantly of different interests and opinions yet we never separate but upon good terms" said Flinders, commenting, "I am as pleasantly situated here at present as a prisoner can well be". However, he concluded his letter with the revelation that he often retired to his little pavilion, flute in hand to play a song which he had sent to his wife: "Ah my beloved, then my heart overleaps the distance of half a world and wholly embraces thee".

Notwithstanding his attachment to his wife, Flinders was also clearly infatuated with the personality of Mme d'Arifat's eldest daughter, Delphine, whom he described as "an extraordinary young lady, possessing a strength of mind, a resolution, and a degree of penetration which few men can boast of; and to these are joined activity, industry and a desire for information". In his life, he confided to Thomi Pitot, he had been fortunate to meet "two extraordinary young women", one of whom was his wife, and that Mlle Delphine now constituted a third. In different circumstances, gushed Flinders, she might have played an important role in history, "ou entre les bienfaiteurs du genre humain, ou entre les heros célebrés". He imagined that she would make "une femme affectionée et une mère excellente. Elle possède ma très-haute considération et mon estime". Pitot did not remark on Flinders' overblown language in his reply, but perhaps the friends were accustomed to complimenting their female acquaintances in this way, for Thomi responded with high praise of his own sister, now Mme Rouillard, who resided at Poudre d'Or. He also informed Flinders that it was in fact his friend Chazal who had first suggested Mme d'Arifat, knowing her to have the pavilions, which were lying empty. Pitot expressed his pleasure that the arrangement was proceeding well.

Towards the end of December 1805, Delphine left to visit her married brother in Flacq, on the other side of the island, and on

New Year's Day, Flinders penned her a note, which, however, he never sent. The letter was full of conflicting sentiments. Flinders had purchased fans for Delphine and her sisters, which, he explained, were token gifts, being aware that 'delicacy' might not permit the acceptance of a present that was of any value. He wrote warmly of his wife: "at the recollection of whom my heart melts within me" and yet betrayed feelings for Delphine, in the lines "remember the expression <u>à jamais,</u> and if the word <u>doucement</u>! escapes your lips, remember the pain it once caused me. Your beauty - but this is the affair of your lover, and therefore no concern of mine".

The pleasures of social interaction in such charming company were, however, no substitute for freedom and as it dawned on Flinders that there was no near prospect of a return to his wife and his work, he became severely depressed in the latter half of 1806. Flinders had planned to invite Ann to join him in the Isle of France but he was dissuaded by his friends and by his own contemplation of the dangers and uncertainties of the journey. The absence of Thomi Pitot in Bourbon, and the departure of his neighbours to spend the cooler months at their town houses exacerbated his melancholy. He wrote petulantly to Thomi in October, "this long absence of yours tires me. ... I have need of your friendly consolation to keep up my spirits: my mind has suffered exceedingly within this month or two past", and to his wife, in November, "I never, even in the Maison Despeaux, experienced such depression". He recovered sufficiently, however, to make a joke of Thomi Pitot's continued absence: "are you, my friend, establishing a house of commerce at Bourbon? Are you making arrangements for your marriage with some worthy and sick citoyenne of Bourbon? or what is it which keeps you so long from your friends?"

The warm-hearted Thomi Pitot wrote to Chazal, urging him to keep the Englishman occupied, and Flinders indeed spent many afternoons at Mondrain, playing music, or 'tric-trac', which he described as "a game something resembling back-gammon" and even contemplating taking a course of instruction in landscape painting from his friend. In fact Thomi was soon to be dabbling in matters of the heart – but as he reported to Flinders, they concerned Labauve d'Arifat rather than himself. In Saint-Denis, he met "the fair one who had so long broken the peace of our friend La Bauve" but was inclined to believe that had he taken his infatuation to its logical matrimonial conclusion, he "would have not enjoyed a constant and uninterrupted felicity".

Flinders' single friends were certainly happier than the Englishman, whose period of separation from his wife was far from over. Edouard, reported Pitot in 1807, "was much in love at Mauritius" and called his brother home from Bourbon, to attend his wedding. He married his niece, Clémence Rouillard, in that year. Charles Desbassayns was also involved in marital negotiations. In August 1807 Flinders informed Captain Bergeret that "the pretty Miss Lise [d'Arifat] has received proposals of marriage from Mr. Charles Desbassayns, the youngest of the Bourbon family of that name: he is an estimable and well informed young man, and tolerably rich. His offer has been accepted, and in January following the marriage is to take place". With his customary graciousness, Flinders found means to compliment Charles' prospective bride: "nature develops itself every day with her; her person is embellished, her manners gain in amiability, and her mind in sentiment… She has pleased without searching to please, but learns daily better to appreciate the value of her conquest. You are to be envied, my dear Sir", he wrote to his friend.

By then, Flinders had another cross to bear. His friendship with Delphine, through a minor and unexplained tiff, cooled dramatically. Several weeks after their 'little quarrel' Flinders complained, "I was the party that had a right to be offended at what was said to me, but wished to pass it over; for which I am punished by opposition and neglect as if the case was the reverse". Matters did not improve, and by September he was writing in his journal: "the conduct of one of my friends in this house has continued to give me much pain these four or five months, my warmest friendship was first attracted by kindness and amiability of conduct almost unparalleled, which is now changed to the opposite, keeping just within the rules of decency". Flinders also observed to his friend Charles Desbassayns, that Delphine "has not recovered from the state of sadness in which you left her: I believe she sheds many tears in secret: she is changed considerably; to me she has been changed more than twelve months. It is but too evident that I no longer possess any place in her friendship, and my regret is proportionate to my loss: it has been one of the bitterest bitter ingredients in my chalice". Flinders' biographers have speculated as to whether Delphine may have been romantically attracted to the Englishman [see, for example, Ingleton: 333] but it is more likely that neither Flinders' morals nor Creole proprieties would have permitted an intimate relationship to develop. Flinders himself had occasion to comment on the modest behaviour of the young, single women – who would not even allow themselves to be accompanied home. Married ladies had more latitude, indeed Flinders was surprised by the conversation of some of his Creole acquaintances: "little slips are spoken of, and laughed at, but do not prevent either one party or the other from being admitted into all societies". Mentioning that Madame Argentil (the divorced wife of M. Dunienville) "frightened our family with a visit" but "conducted herself with moderation, and went away early the following morning" Flinders does not, however, reveal what it was in that lady's conduct that alarmed her hosts. When young, unmarried ladies occasionally 'slipped up', this did not escape his attention. Thus after congratulating the daughter of a neighbour on her impending marriage, Flinders does not fail to mention in his journal, some months later, that her child was born "13 days less than 9 months after marriage".

Certainly, for Flinders, the carefree days of learning to waltz with the d'Arifat girls seemed to be over. At another dance party, given by the Chazals in May 1808, he did not participate, and finding noone to converse with, complained "my evening passed dull enough". Yet, despite the coolness of Delphine, Flinders had by now become totally integrated into the French Creole way of life. He spoke their language fluently, and thought nothing of whiling away afternoons picnicking with the Chazals "à manger un carrie dans les bois" as he put it. He was fully part of the d'Arifat family, and in January 1808 attended the simple and touching marriage ceremony of Charles Desbassayns and Lise d'Arifat, conducted by the abbé Flageollet. Most of the ceremony was in Latin, Flinders recorded, "the two contracting parties kneeling the whole time". Lise and Charles settled in Bourbon after their marriage and Flinders often sent letters to them. In December 1808, learning that they were expecting a child, he wrote to the couple:

> *You will scarcely devine a thought which strikes me, and which, if you join in it, will ensure me what I have much at heart: to be never forgotten by my friends at Mauritius and Bourbon. It is this. I suppose that your first child will be a son; and if you give him more than one name, I beg of you as a proof of your desire to continue our friendship to the last, that his second, third or fourth baptismal name, may be Flinders…. if your son bears my name I shall consider him as my God-son, and ever take an affectionate interest in his welfare.*

This was yet another demonstration of the importance that Flinders attached to the notion of friendship, and the degree to which he considered himself close to the d'Arifat family

Charles Desbassayns readily agreed to this proposal, and Flinders' response, in Jan 1809, was to tell the couple "I have already conceived an affection for the dear child, and should circumstances determine you to send him to England one day, it will be the greatest proof of friendship you can give me, to confide him to my charge". In May 1809, Lise gave birth to a healthy girl, but in August Charles wrote to Flinders that "à l'aide du ciel un de mes fils portera le nom de Flinder et quoiqu'il en arrive, je porterai toujours ce nom dans mon coeur".

It was certainly Flinders' wish that his extraordinary rapport with his Mauritian friends, and in particular the Pitot and d'Arifat families, should endure after his departure, and he consequently spent much time, after his return to England, corresponding with them and exchanging family news. Mme d'Arifat also wrote frequently - after the conquest of the islands she visited her children in Bourbon – and joyfully wrote of her reunion with her children there and her delight with Pauline, her grandchild.

Charles Desbassayns and one of the family estates - at St Gilles

She also sent him news of her sons Aristide – who planned to join the navy – and of André. Charles had taken an important official post offered by the new British government which left Lise "desolée ... elle aurait bien préféré que Charles vécut uniquement pour elle, pour elever ses enfans, ce bonheur paisible, sa jolie campagne, il faut abandonner tout cela, habiter la ville". The many letters from the islands testified to new alliances and to new lodgers. Flinders learnt that Frederic Pitot was to marry Elie de Mouhy, and that Le Refuge had another English tenant – an Indian officer, visiting to recover his health. In August 1811, she added "parlant mariage, il s'en est fait une assez grande quantité de vos compatriotes avec des demoiselles françaises", and a couple of months later, wrote with news of Labauve's conjugal felicity with Delphine Perichon. Flinders was no doubt also pleased to learn that Charles Desbassayns had a son – who was named Henry Flinders.

In 1812 it was Flinders' turn to inform his friends of the forthcoming birth of his child. Charles Desbassayns responded: "I claim from that young Flinder his friendship for his name sake of Bourbon. I do not lose sight my friend of your offers to take charge of my boy". Sophie and Delphine were the topic of letters in the following year, when their marriages to M. Charreton and the 39 year old M. Pailleux were announced – Pailleux was described by his friend Charles as "a man of honour, of sense and as much mildness and vertue as he is possessed of resolution and strength of character". Delphine's tendency to be imperious, had softened, wrote Charles. Aristide's navy career was abruptly terminated: "nous l'avons placé en qualité de pilotin sur un de nos vaisseaux, … après 24 heures de séjour à bord il s'est trouvé incommodé, a debarqué et a repris une autre place dans le commissariat à Bourbon". The Chazal family had returned from a lengthy trip to India.

Flinders, with a letter to Mme d'Arifat lying unfinished on his desk, received one from Labauve informing him that she had passed away in August 1812. Charles also had disquieting news about Flinders' young namesake. "My boy is strong, stout, healthy, roguish and somewhat odd. He does not appear to be very sensible though quick enough for a lad of his age being little more than 2 and a half" he wrote. Indeed, young Henry Flinders was to die young, before he could make any mark on the world.

Flinders maintained his correspondence with his Mauritian friends until his own premature death in 1814. His last advice on marriage, however, delivered to his English friend William Fitzwilliam Owen, a fellow former prisoner on the Isle of France, decidedly negatived the prospects of Anglo-Creole alliances. Owen had evidently romanced the daughter of M. Foisy, while at the Isle of France, and in January 1812, wrote to Flinders in his usual jocular style: "I esteemed myself half happy that I was prevented from proceeding to the Isle of France since French wives, however admired, are something out of repute. But the letters of Foisy and his family seem to imply that I am not yet out of the scrape, if then you should hear that I bring a wife home with me remember that it will be one of your finest admirers although she knew you not". Flinders did not take the matter so lightly, admonishing his friend:

Now my dear Sir, a word of advice to you upon marriage. If you marry a foreigner, especially a creole, you will entail upon yourself many inconveniences. Of all the creoles returned from the Isle of France, there is not one who does not sigh day and night after their natal spot. The father of a family, arrived not many months in France writes to me "Malheur à l'Européen qui s'entourent des créoles". His wife and daughter talk of nothing, think of nothing but Mauritius and there is not a fruit, even to the miserable guava, which is not preferred to the best fruits of France. But perhaps you are already married; and I have already made an enemy of Miss Foisy; but no, she has too much sense not to see, that my advice points not to her, but to the impossibility of a creole being happy in Europe. If you be not married, stop, by all means, till you arrive here.

Flinders knew well the charmed life of the Mauritian elite – it had after all worked its own spell on him – and was no doubt thinking of the woes of his friend Sauveget whose wife and daughter were born on the island and who pressured him to organize their return to Mauritius in 1813 (see p. 155).

Owen evidently followed Flinders' advice, for he never brought Mlle Foisy home as his wife – indeed, as Hugh Hope's letters show (Chapter 1), he had forgotten the Creole belle almost before the island was out of sight – becoming enamoured instead of a Miss Butler, who was aboard the *Harriet*. However, it was to Martha Evans that Owen eventually plighted his troth - in 1818. They had two daughters and he died at the venerable age of 84, in 1857.

If the Mlle Foisy with whom Owen was engaged, was the same young lady – Clementine Foisy - who afterwards found and tragically lost an English fiancé, Archibald Litchfield in 1817, then she was indeed unlucky in love. Travel accounts describe her solitary visits to his graveside each evening at dusk, and she died a relatively young spinster. Delphine Pailleux, née d'Arifat fared better – she lived to a ripe old age, dying in Bourbon in 1875. She outlived her sister Sophie – Charles' wife - by one year, and was buried in the St Paul cemetery, where the inscription on her tombstone can still be read today.

4. The Slave Economy and Society

Flinders came to the Isle of France at a time when anti-slave trade agitation was beginning to build at home, but there is no reason to suppose that he himself had any strong feelings against a system that, in his day, was not only legal, but common in many parts of the world. His friends on the island were principally of the slave-owning class themselves, and indeed his relationship with Thomi Pitot would lead the Englishman to follow that merchant's defence in a slave-trading case. On reading, in 1807, of a French plot to excite the West Indian slaves to revolt, he commented "this, if correct, is an atrocity which merits general detestation" demonstrating that his sympathies lay with the property owners rather than with the rabble rousers. At the same time, Flinders' writings indicate that he was a caring and sensitive individual, and, placed as he was in a unique position to observe the mores and customs of a slave-owning society, it is interesting to investigate his own dealings with, and comments upon, the persons of colour, slave or free, which whom he came into contact on the island.

It is clear that Flinders himself used the services of slaves throughout his time at the Isle of France. Indeed, a slave was practically thrust upon him, towards the end of 1804, in the person of Toussaint. This young boy was formerly a slave of Walter Robertson - a British surgeon employed in the Indian service, and a former fellow prisoner at the Maison Despeaux. When Robertson was given an opportunity to depart on an American ship bound for Salem, he was obliged to leave the boy behind – as Flinders commented "the good Quakers of that place not allowing a black man to be brought to their town: the poor boy is left to go to England with me". In fact, Flinders did not take Toussaint with him when he eventually left, although the boy evidently accompanied him to Le Refuge. Indeed, after the departure of his English servants, it may be inferred that Flinders made use of slaves for domestics – for his final journey to the port, he took Toussaint and another slave with him. On 10 June 1810, he wrote "sent away my little black servant

Toussaint with a letter to Madame D'Arifat and a recompense, and took Wm. Herman, a seaman late of the *Sea-flower* as a servant". Toussaint therefore remained as a slave with the d'Arifat family.

Once liberated from his port prison, Flinders quickly discovered how indispensable slaves were in the transport of goods and persons across the island. Whenever he took a long journey, a slave would invariably carry his trunk. Messages to and from the port were generally taken by slaves, and it was not unusual for them to carry the female colonists in palanquins, while the men would ride horses. Thus, on one occasion, Flinders recounts how he and the d'Arifat family travelled to Vacouas: "Madame D'Arifat in a palanquin, Mr. Labauve, myself, and Miss Delphine on horseback, and followed by about thirty blacks, carrying the luggage".

Travelling around the island – helped by slaves

After the departure of Elder, Flinders also relied on slaves to undertake relatively sensitive missions. He sent Faro to the port on one occasion to learn from the Commissary of Prisoners of a cartel whether he would get permission to leave with him, telling the latter: "you can keep him, at least, until Sunday at noon; ordering him to come to you as often and when you judge proper". And, in 1808, when he decided to create a lookout for himself at Tamarin – with a view of escaping aboard an English ship, he was helped by two slaves lent to him by Chazal. They spent the whole day with Flinders employed in "cutting a path in the woods to the point whence the bay of Tamarinds and that part of the coast is visible".

The Tourelle of Tamarin – Flinders' Lookout

It is important to note, however, that Flinders happily paid the slaves for services carried out on his behalf, and, when he employed them, took care not only to offer them generous wages, but to ensure that their owner – usually Mme d'Arifat - was not unduly inconvenienced. For example, in December 1807, when he sent three trunks to the port, in expectation of an early departure from the island, he took advantage of a Sunday when the slaves were at liberty either to rest or to work on their own account, to hire them for this service. He offered them "half a dollar each, with an addition in promise if they return early, for at this season the maize nearly ripe, requires to be guarded in the night, and I have too much obligation and friendship for my hostess not to avoid putting her to any inconveniences". When he planned to escape, in March 1808, Flinders left some money to recompense no fewer than 6 of

Mme d'Arifat's domestics, whom he said "have been in the habitude of serving me".

Thus, in his transactions with slaves, there is no reason to suppose that Flinders treated them any differently than he would a manual labourer from his own country. Certainly, the tasks that slaves were called upon to carry out at the Isle of France indicate that many were trusted employees, who handled money and valuables. In certain respects, he was regularly indebted to their superior knowledge. For example, when he set off on excursions, Alaise, the black servant of Mme d'Arifat, was frequently his guide.

The confidence placed in the slaves is demonstrated by their role in corsair ships and in the manning of the island's coastal fortifications. Flinders reported in August 1809 that General Decaen had ordered "a regiment of 650 blacks to be raised by a levy of 1 in 20 upon all the male slaves between 15 and 25 years possessed by the inhabitants". His friend Labauve d'Arifat consequently "conducted all the slaves he possessed between the ages required, from hence to the port at the Black River where an officer made choice of 3 for the new regiment". Only a month later, however, it was learnt that the slaves of Bourbon had risen up in revolt. Flinders was told that some of them requested arms from the English cruisers then surrounding the island, but Commodore Rowley, leading the squadron, kept them on board his ship and later returned them to their masters. Despite the suppression of the revolt, the news cooled support for Decaen's slave regiment, which was abandoned.

Flinders soon realized that the Isle of France was a country of some social and ethnic complexity. A prosperous class of free coloureds lived in circumstances not far removed from, and sometimes much better than those of their working class white counterparts. In August 1805, for example, Flinders called with the overseer, Peter Salomon, at the house of Jean Barrow, to enquire if that gentleman would supply the Englishman with poultry, vegetables, eggs and milk. Jean, as Flinders noted, was a 'free black man', who was himself a landed proprietor and slave-owner: "Jean Barrow seemed to have a tolerably good house and plantation, with 25 slaves; and he had a large family of half one-third-white children of his own having a mulattresse for his wife". Flinders also spoke appreciatively of the "good black overseer" of the d'Arifats, who went out of his way to ensure that all the Englishman's wants were supplied. And when he was informed that his release had been ordered from France he did not fail to impart the good news to his black acquaintance: "Called upon our honest black neighbour Jean Paul in passing, to tell him of the news I had received, at which he expressed great pleasure and many good wishes; he said he had often prayed to God for me".

Flinders' intellectual curiosity about his temporary island home naturally extended to the culture and background of the slave population. While still in Port Louis, Flinders had occasion to observe the holidays celebrated by the slave and free coloured residents of the capital. On New Year's Day 1805, he wrote:

It surprised me to find the lower class of people here making a festival of the new years day. The band of musick was playing in the streets a considerable part of the night and all the black people and servants were running about in the morning calling banana, banana, with flowers in their hands which they presented to all their masters and his friends, and whomsoever else would take them, and demanded money for them, from a trois-sous piece to a piastre.

The word Flinders heard as 'banana' was undoubtedly the Creole form of the French greeting 'bonne année'.

When Flinders experienced his second New Year on the island, he was no longer surprised at the celebrations of the slaves. As he explained in his journal entry for 1st January 1806:

This day is the greatest holiday that the slaves in this island have throughout the year. They were collected from two or three plantations at a little distance from hence, and were drumming upon their tom-tom, singing, firing muskets, and perhaps dancing all the night preceding and all the day nearly. At breakfast time the whole or greater part of Mad. D'Arifat's slaves, old and young, came to pay their respects to their mistresses family and present them with nose-gays, and to wish them a bonne-année. I took this opportunity of making little presents to those of the slaves who had done me any service and threw some pence amongst the children to scramble for. ...

In the latter part of the day, the greater part of the black-men were drunk, but some few took the occasion of paying distant visits to their distant friends, and it is said that some of them have been known to walk twenty leagues, from New Years morning after breakfast, to the next morning at daylight when they are obliged to be at home at their work.

Flinders' distribution of money to slaves of the neighbourhood became a New Year custom – the 1st January 1809 again saw him hand out 20 dollars "amongst the slaves of the habitants, amounting to 60 including a number of young children". By the New Year of 1810 – his last on the island – the sum Flinders expended had risen to "30 dollars, in return for their nosegays and good wishes".

A slave dance

Flinders lived in close proximity to the slaves of the d'Arifat habitation as the plan of Le Refuge indicates. Their accommodation was generally in the form of thatched huts: no match for the severe weather that the island experienced during the cyclone season (November to April). Flinders had the occasion to observe the damage that such gales could inflict. On the night of Thursday 20th February 1806, he reported: "the wind blew excessively hard, so that there was danger of the house and our pavilions being overset". The following morning, Flinders walked out to survey the damage: "the garden, where there are two fish ponds, fed by the river, was all covered with water. The huts of the slaves, fowl-houses, graineries and almost every building covered with thatch, was unroofed".

Plan of Le Refuge, showing double row of slave houses to the left of the main house, and Flinders' pavilions [after Ingleton]

A year later, in early 1807, Flinders again observed the destructive power of the seasonal cyclones. At Le Refuge:

almost the whole of the maize upon the ground was destroyed: the manioc obliged to be taken out of the ground half grown, to save it from rotting. Many fruit trees blown up by the roots ... the huts of the negroes uncovered.

108

He reported that in both the Isles of France and Bourbon hundreds of slaves had been killed, when their homes were swept away, while the price of foodstuffs was driven sky-high. "Many of the inhabitants unable to give any food whatever to their slaves, left them to search for nourishment where they could", he wrote, explaining that numerous robberies and even murders were committed "solely in order to obtain wherewith to satisfy resistless hunger". In this context, we can understand better why Flinders attributed the disappearance of his cat, Trim, while he was at the port, to 'catophagi', speculating that the "unsuspecting animal was stewed and eaten by some hungry black slave".

One of the local solutions to the food shortages was in the cultivation of maize, and Flinders immediately saw the benefit that this foodstuff could bring to English settlements such as Port Jackson. Consequently he closely observed the slaves at work in its preparation:

> *the negress or Negro [sits] upon his hams with three or four pieces of cloths, bags or sacks spread around him, a sack of maize by his side and basket in his hand. He takes a convenient quantity, perhaps a pound or two at a time into his basket, and by moving it back from side to side, with a slight movement forwards, he makes the light husks rise at the top in the fore part, this is thrown aside upon one of the cloths.*

Flinders even contemplated taking "two or three handy slaves from this colony to Port Jackson to teach the art", believing that it would soon be widely adopted there. On another outing, he noticed that the fields were covered with 'sweet potato', "a root of great utility to the nourishment of the slaves ... because the hurricanes can do it no injury".

He also had many opportunities to hear the Creole language, which he remarked was both used and "apparently invented by the negro slaves". He avidly read a copy of the story of the Marquis de Caraba, in a Creole translation, commenting that it revealed not only the "particular genius of their language, but also shews much of their character". It seems clear from such comments that Flinders both admired the ingenuity of the black slave population and noticed their cultural specifities. His acquaintance with Barthelemy de Froberville, who had spent much time editing accounts of Madagascar, sparked his interest in the natives of that island, and led him to interview a Malagasy slave woman in 1808:

> *Questioned a slave Amboilambe here, relative to various points in the journals of M. M. Mayeur and Dumaine. She appears to have quitted the country about 1768 or 70, some years before Mr. Mayeur arrived, and gave the name of the principal king being different from him, but the other king she named the same. She confirmed the horrible fact of the Hovas or Amboilambes digging deep holes in their houses which they cover over, and then inviting travellers to accept hospitality they contrive to make him fall in; he is then seized, and bound, and sold into slavery. This negress is black (or dark Sambou) with woolly hair, but at first almost denied she was of the cast Magnissoutre, but afterwards acknowledged it.*

Flinders 'anthropological fieldwork' would not pass muster today, but testify to his readiness to interact with, and learn from, the slave population of the island.

He had also read – in Grant's *History of Mauritius*, published in 1801, the true story of the Malagasy Princess Bety, who handed her dominion – St Mary's Island - to the French and settled on the Isle of France. She also resided in Plaines Wilhems, dying while Flinders was still there. He did not meet her, but understood that she "left a pretty estate to some mulattoes who are called her nephews...The slaves of the planters in the neighbourhood, who came from her part of Madagascar were in the habit of asking permission from their masters to visit her on a Sunday, and it is said they were always kindly received, and seldom returned without some present".

In May 1806, Flinders had the occasion to observe the traces of another black community on the island, when he breakfasted at the house of a Mr Ducasse, and was taken to see nearby caves. A settlement of between 30 and 50 maroon slaves had been discovered at this place some years earlier. He was informed that the maroons' hide out had been discovered and reported to the troops who shot their sentry, surprising the maroons – who slept during the day – and capturing the remainder. In their cavern, "besides a few musquets and other arms, with a small quantity of ammunition, little else was found than a bag of dollars, some pieces of cloth and a provision of maize and a slaughtered goat". This story was not merely apocryphal, since Flinders saw the evidence himself:

> The skull of their captain who was said to possessed of much cunning and audacity was at this time lying upon a stone at the entrance of the cave and for the narrowness of the front and large extent of the back part of the head, was the most singularly formed cranium I ever saw: the semi-circular little enclosures formed with small stones by the sides of the cavern, once the sleeping places of these wretches, also existed, as they had left them; owing apparently to the superstition of the black, and the policy and disgust of the white visitors to the cavern.

These caverns are located at St Pierre between Bambous and Tamarin [Barnwell: 37].

The presence of such dangerously disaffected slaves, and the fact that slaves were being imported to the island while Flinders was there, only enters his narrative incidentally. In September 1805, for example, while on a visit to the Mare aux Vacoas, Flinders passed a plantation that belonged to a ship's commander, "who at present was gone to Madagascar to procure slaves to work his plantation, which was newly settled". In 1807, he recounts an incident in which "a strong black newly arrived from Mozambique" makes an appearance. Flinders noticed him because he was the only slave of the habitation who was able to return one night, after a bout of heavy rain, by swimming across the Rivière du Rempart. On another occasion, he remarked that a cyclone had caused a ship carrying 300 slaves from Mozambique to be wrecked, but that the 'cargo' was saved.

Flinders was certainly aware of the importance of the slave economy to the colonists, and of its political implications. When the English occupation was imminent, and he was given an opportunity – at the Cape of Good Hope – to give an account of the colonists, and of their situation, he voiced their concerns on this issue. As he wrote to Mme d'Arifat on 24 August 1810:

J'ai parlé des craintes qu'on avait rélativement aux esclaves, et au port; et j'ai trouvé lieu de croire, que tout se passera à l'avantage de l'Isle de France; excepté peut-être que l'importation future d'esclaves sera nécessairement défendue d'après les lois fines d'Angleterre.

Soon after his return to England, the slave question – with its partisans and opponents - continued to be of concern to Flinders, who, through the Pitots, became directly involved in a slave-trading case. In December 1810, Thomi had informed him of the details:

Un charmant vaisseau construit par nous sur les gabaris de la corvette l'Entreprenant et prêt à être expedié en aventurier pour France sous le nom de l'Eclair se trouve compris dans la capture de tous les batiments sous couleurs dans notre port ... une perte assez lourde.

The celebrated abolitionist, Zachary Macauley, brought the case, with two others, to the attention of the authorities in Britain, claiming that "a slave trade attended with circumstances of peculiar cruelty" was being carried on from Madagascar to the Isle of France. Among the proofs cited was the case of the brig *L'Eclair*, captured in September 1811, and "built at Ile de France, and fitted out by the owners Charles Pitot, Edward Pitot and Thomas Pitot, merchants of Port Louis, to trade in cattle with Madagascar". Macauley asserted that when the vessel was captured "she was found to have 126 blacks on board hidden in a confined space almost without air". Coincidentally, from Flinders' perspective, one of the ships cited in Macauley's complaint had been captured by Captain Lynne – an ex-POW whom he had known on the island. The then British governor of Mauritius, Farquhar, however, supported the owners of the ship, and asserted their innocence, taking an opposing stance from Lynne. When Pitot wrote to Flinders about his own case – which his English friend was following on his behalf – he vehemently decried the propagandists:

> *Nous sommes toujours fort avides des nouvelles relatives à notre malheureuse affaire de noirs et nous craignons que malgré l'indignité de la conduite de nos adversaires et la justice de notre cause, le violent prejugé qui existe en Angleterre contre tout ce qui tient à la traite n'influence même le respectable magistrat qui doit prononcer dans cette affaire.*

Flinders evidently took charge of this case for Pitot for he reported to his friend in November 1812 that he had made out a statement of the case and placed it in the hands of Messrs Gostling, proctors in the Admiralty Court. In January 1813 he received from Sir Joseph Banks, the copy of an opinion of the Attorney and Solicitor General on another case similar to Pitot's which ruled on the application of the anti slave trade laws to newly conquered colonies. Flinders considered that "the construction seems favourable to your taking your slaves to the Cape ... but it is not decisive". During 1813 Flinders sat through several hearings of the case in the Admiralty Court, reporting periodically to Pitot. In July he mentioned that "Mr. Gostling seems to think the case of *l'Industrie* to be most favourable of the three". Flinders also used his own local knowledge to advance his friend's cause. On learning that the anti-slavery activist Mr Brougham was intending to "enlarge upon the cruelty of confining such a number of slaves on board the small vessels *L'Eclair* etc. for a long sea passage", Flinders informed Pitot's counsel that the passage from the West Indies to Africa was by no means comparable to the journey between Madagascar and Mauritius, which was only 160 leagues, and took from 7 to 14 days: "a comparison of the cruelty in one case, cannot therefore be applied to the other with justice", he wrote.

The case of *l'Eclair* was the last to be decided, but based on the decisions already made, Flinders wrote "I hope you will get the vessel and bullocks, and such slaves as can be proved to have been purchased before the capitulation: the rest will certainly be lost". By 1814, Flinders' worsening health obliged him to give up the case, and Pitot suggested placing it with a London firm, Morris and Renny. This was carried out by Mrs Flinders after the death of her husband.

In this case, Flinders was evidently supporting the position of his friend, nevertheless the record of his dealings with the slaves and free blacks that he met on the island, is an adequate testament both to his own humane attitudes and to the liberality with which his closest friends treated their domestic and plantation servants.

Conflict Onshore & at Sea

From his vantage point on the Isle of France, and his privileged relationship with the colonists, Flinders was able to provide an interesting, if fragmented, perspective on the evolving conflict in the Indian Ocean. His letters and journal entries concerning the activities of the French privateers and the progress of the English blockade effectively communicate the fears and hopes of the opposing sides, and offer a dramatic, personal insight into colonial life during the Napoleonic wars.

Flinders was supplied with much of his information concerning the political situation through Thomi Pitot, who, whilst a staunchly patriotic Frenchman, was a friend to anyone in need. Pitot's interventions are all the more remarkable, when one considers that he was fitting out the ships that took the prizes, and then seeking to make the imprisonment of those who were captured as amenable as possible! This was however, still an age of gentlemanly warfare, and ships' captains often displayed great concern for their defeated counterparts.

Initially, Flinders' interest in the British squadron that periodically cruised off the island, was principally directed towards his own liberation – whilst still at the Garden Prison in the capital he imagined that boats coming in shore were there to demand his release. This hope soon faded however, particularly when Flinders learnt that a demand made for him had been rejected on the ground that he was not considered a 'prisoner of war'. He began to observe more dispassionately the tactics – and their failings – of the blockading squadron. He noted early that the British tended to avoid molesting neutral ships, and did not interfere with coasting vessels: "the squadron under Admiral Linois seems to be their principal object, and of course they take all French ships coming to the island". Flinders and his fellow inmates frequently heard the sound of 'cannonading' as the cruisers engaged in skirmishes with French vessels endeavouring to get in and out of the port, but could not help noticing how many prizes managed, notwithstanding, to avoid the cruisers.

In October 1804, for example, he reported, "it appears that the contre-amiral Linois has got into the Grand Port with three prizes, either unperceived or unimpeded by our cruizers". It was soon obvious that the French knew the English routine too well, for no sooner had the cruising squadron sailed off, then the French prizes began to come in. In the middle of 1806 Flinders noted that the British cruisers had "reduced the Isle of France to great scarcity of grain, by preventing the arrivals from Bourbon, Madagascar and India" but "the ships were scarcely out of sight when the vessels loaded with grain and flour began to arrive, and in the fortnight that no cruizers were off the island, no less than 8 so charged came into port". The fortuity of their timing led the inhabitants to be "tempted to believe their island under the peculiar protection of Providence". The taking of the *Warren Hastings*, which he valued at no less than a million dollars, had by a similar twist of fate, saved the government from a financial crisis. Later, noting that a French ship had succeeded in entering Black River he commented "the cruizers keep to windward generally, and thus they miss the greater part of the ships that come to the island, especially as they keep so near as that the signals on the mountains shew their place".

Flinders frequently calculated the value of the captured ships and was consequently under no illusions as to the damage inflicted on British commercial interests by the Isle of France privateers. In December 1806, when *La Piémontaise* arrived in port, Flinders commented, "this ship has taken, or done injury to the English commerce, to the amount of a million and a half of dollars, within the last eight months!" Flinders soon wearied of the incessant tally of prizes taken back and forth, particularly when he saw how they affected the interests of his friends. In November 1808, learning of the fortunes and adversities of both sides, and that *La Jeune Claire*, belonging to Mr Pitot had been taken, he commented, "It is thus that the individuals of two nations tear each other, without doing any essential service to the general cause of either".

The prisoners of war were not entirely dependent on news brought by outsiders, for the arrival of an English squadron was usually broadcast by means of a red flag hoisted on Signal Hill at the port. But the details were usually supplied by fellow prisoners departing on leave, or more circumspectly, by their neutral and French friends at the port. Flinders' servant, John Elder, could also be relied upon, in his daily shopping trips, to pick up relevant information. In January 1806, for example, he brought back news of a projected attack on the *Pitt* by *La Semillante* and *La Bellone*, and Flinders betrayed a certain English pride, when discussing the matter in a letter to Thomi Pitot. The superiority of the men and arms of the French attacking force, he contended "montre bien l'appréciation faite par votre gouvernement de l'adresse et de la bravoure de mes compatriotes ... j'attends avec impatience votre conte du combat et du résultat". On learning that the attack had not taken place, he acknowledged, however, "the greater part of the people of the island, as well as myself, are glad that the Pitt is gone away without any action having taken place".

The Pitt

Naturally Flinders also heard news of local politics, some of which revealed the difficulties entailed by the island's remoteness. He pointed out for example, that when the anniversary of the establishment of the French republic was celebrated with a large dinner party at Government House, "there was some embarrassment from the uncertainty of Bonaparte's election to the imperial dignity". Information of the progress of the war in Europe also trickled through. In February 1806, Pitot passed onto him the news of Bonaparte's victory over Archduke Ferdinand, "and of a naval victory over our fleet, in which the gallant Lord Nelson was killed".

The Battle of Pulo-Aur

In fact, Bonaparte had proclaimed himself Emperor on 14th May 1804 but his dream of invading England had come to an abrupt end with Nelson's victory off Cape Trafalgar on 21st October 1805. He was more successful against Austria and Russia at Austerlitz, and defeated Prussia at Jena the following year. Napoleon next embarked on a war of attrition with England – his invasion of Spain and Portugal was designed to squeeze British trade – but this was a vital miscalculation – embroiling him in the 6-year long Peninsula War. In the Indian Ocean, the French tried to block British trade links between China and India, but the decisive February 1804 battle of Pulo-Aur went Britain's way. Admiral Peter Rainier, Commander in Chief of British forces in the East, next turned his attention to French privateering – which had been a more successful irritant to British trade. His blockade of the Isle of France was ordered in June 1804. In early 1806 a British force captured the Cape of Good Hope. "What news the prisoner had of these events came to him in bits and pieces, months out of date, largely from his French friends on the island. Yet, however eager he may have been for it, his private world was and continued so detached that the intelligence made scarcely any difference" [Mack: 189].

Flinders was at times exasperated by the conflicting reports he received of the war situation. In August 1806, his Swiss friend Johann Boand brought news – via ships from Tranquebar and India - that peace was much talked of. A few days later, he expostulated, "What contradictory reports! War is now said to be declared by Sweden and Prussia against France".

Flinders and Pitot also discussed the prospects of peace and differed in their views. In a letter to his friend dated 18th December 1806, Flinders wrote:

You seem to think, my dear friend, that a peace is not unlikely to soon terminate this disastrous contest between our two nations; but however much I desire it, the difficulties that stand in the way of peace, make me almost hopeless of its soon taking place. The ascendancy of Bonaparte over one half of the European continent and his determined enmity against England leave but little prospect of peace so long as the latter shall preserve her independence, and to obtain it at such a price I could never consent.

Turning his attention back to the activities of the privateers, Flinders commented on the dubious scruples of the French captains who brought in 'Moorish' ships despite having no quarrel with the nations they represented: "but they are rich, and they are brought in on suspicion of either being English or connected with with merchants of India. ... they are sequestred until the French government shall decide whether they are to be prizes or not: it is scarcely to be doubted that right will be on the strongest side. The moors will get nothing back, the privateers probably nothing, the government will keep all".

In the light of these outrages, Flinders found it curious that the French newspapers were "filled with invectives against the English and their tyranny on the seas, whilst the frigates and privateers of the island are making prizes of almost all the Arab ships they can meet with". He was fast learning something of the power of propaganda, and of the best way of dealing with it, commenting sardonically, "credit must be granted to the French editors for qualifying so neatly the faults of their own government, and exaggerating those of their enemies ... At first, they made my anger rise, but at present they make me laugh; they are become nauseous even to the greater part of the French themselves, at least here".

However, he suffered from what he viewed as "the efforts of the French government and gazetteers to render the British government odious by misrepresentations" when he became embroiled in arguments with friends such as Chazal who were inclined to believe reports of injustices prosecuted against their compatriots. After an especially unpleasant incident, he wrote:

Had a violent dispute with Chazal, who reproached the English government with injustice and inhumanity in a most prejudiced manner, and even with crimes that I shewed him it was the French and not the English governmnent that had committed them.... I think, that if there is a second person in the island who would have treated me as general DeCaën has done, notwithstanding the kindness and hospitality I have personally received from Chazal, it is he who would be capable of it.

These were harsh words, but the ill-feeling would not endure for long. Within days Flinders was again socializing with the family. The incident nevertheless, revealed the difficulty for both sides to remain indifferent to the war of propaganda and enmity constantly besieging them.

It is certain also that Pitot and Flinders differed widely in their political views, but this was never allowed by either man to in any way affect their frienship. As Flinders wrote to Pitot in February 1808, "Oh comme je desire que tous les Français et les Anglais étaient dans les mêmes sentiments les uns pour les autres que vous et moi. Alors la paix pourrait régner en Europe, et nous n'aurions d'autres contestations que celles de l'amitié, des arts, et des sciences". Flinders grew to bear the attacks made on his nation's politics with some equanimity. In January 1810, he reported, for example, "Mr. and Mrs. Chevreau gave a dinner to the neighbours on the anniversary of their marriage. Was as usual attacked upon politics".

With Charles Desbassayns, however, he could be more open, as the men shared a dislike for Napoleon. In April 1808, from his Rivière des Pluies estate, for example, Charles penned the following lines to his English friend:

Ce Brigand, cette Canaille de Corse, tend à rendre les hommes Egoistes. On est bien malheureux, ou du moins on a bien à souffrir de detester et mépriser ce Polisson comme il le mérite. J'attends, je soupire après le moment où le bon dieu voudra bien l'appeler à lui et d'ici là je voudrois avoir mon esprit politique ou mon sentiment d'homme en lethargie.

In a letter to Colonel Kerjean, dated 11 March 1807, Flinders displayed what was to become his characteristic attitude to the war: "I see with much regret, that all present hopes of peace are at an end ... This is a severe blow to the quiet part of mankind, and to me in particular; for it becomes every day more and more evident, that I am not destined to see my family and my country, or resume my geographical labours until our chiefs shall be pleased to release us from the scourge, with which the two nations seem to be equally afflicted". Of course, a certain pride in his nation was never effaced in Flinders. A discussion of American politics brought forth the following exclamation from him in a letter to Thomi Pitot: "Is not our little England an astonishing island? No nation upon earth has ever extended its colonies so widely and with so much success".

By late 1808 Flinders still saw little prospect of peace, and had become almost fatalistic. As he advised his friend Charles Desbassayns, "the best way for us, is to leave the affair to Providence, and make ourselves as happy as we can without peace". Yet he could not resist turning again and again to discussion of events in Europe, his mood swinging between the hope that Bonaparte's star was waning in France, and the fear that he might succeed: "is it possible that the French nation will quietly see itself sacrificed, to prosecute the insatiate ambition of a Corsican?" he asked Charles on one occasion.

St. Denis, capital of Bourbon island

During 1809, the effect of the war began to be felt more directly than ever in the islands. In August Flinders informed Charles that the blockade was now controlling the port with a new strictness, and the attention of the colonists became concentrated on the likelihood of a British attack on their own islands. Around this time, rumours began to be heard on the Isle of France, of a British expedition being mounted, and in October, news of an assault against St. Paul in Bourbon began to filter through. The details were sketchy, however, and Flinders commented, "everyone makes suppositions according to what he desires, or fears, and these suppositions are soon given out as facts". The feeling of insecurity was such that Decaen, through Colonel Monistrol, warned Flinders against his tendency to make excursions, "a considerable distance from the habitation of Madame d'Arifat" and ordered him to remain on the plantation.

That evening, out walking, notwithstanding, Flinders met a soldier from Black River who declared that the English were in possession of St. Paul, that "general de Brulie, the governor had destroyed himself, and that the inhabitants had not sought to make any resistance". Labauve, returning from the port with Mr Sornay, confirmed the news of the assault on the sister island.

Soon afterwards, Charles Desbassayns' letter would provide interesting details of the incident as he experienced it. He wrote that he had been making plans to entertain some English prisoners at the family property in St Gilles, when:

> *la carronade commença qui mit fin à toutes ces visites ... les matelots de la Caroline ivres des boissons volées, tirant sans distinction sur blancs et noirs des deux nations vos compatriotes declarerent que leurs intentions étoient de se rendre à St Denis dans 2 jours pour l'attaquer croyant leur force de 1800 hommes et certaine de leur réussite tant par le nombre que par la volonté prononcée des habitans de ne pas se battre. Je crus indispensable de me rendre ici afin que dans le cas d'attaque nous puissions prévenir au moins le désordre que j'avois vu à St Paul, désordre qui auroit entrainé la ruine de la colonie sans la loyauté du Colonel Kiting, du Commodore Rowly et les autres officiers. .. je me mis en route à 2 heures du matin en défis des matelots et autres brigands .. j'arrivai ici sans accidents la veille que ce pauvre General Desbrulys se détruisit en raison des clameurs sansculotiques qu'il trouva dans le Conseil de guerre, sa mort fut le signal des troubles politiques, une secte sanguinaire assoupie depuis longtems mais non éteinte réveillant d'anciennes animosités se mit bientôt à montrer au doigt ceux qu'ils appelèrent Anglomanes, les fins les plus infames furent bientôt vomis par cette secte revolutionnaire d'abord ils décidèrent dans leur sainte ardeur que l'on devoit decimer St Paul, ensuite ils ne demandèrent que 50 têtes et devenant moins avides, ils n'en demanderent que 20 des principaux de cette colonie, leur râge se deploya dans des demandes plus ou moins inhumaines... Des listes de Souscription bientôt signées et envoyées au gouvernment d'ici qui eut la bassesse de les reçevoir, d'autres ont été envoyées au Général de camp qui eut le bon esprit de leur donner le*

mépris qu'elles meritoient … pour moi on me fit même
l'honneur de me désigner comme Chef Conspirateur".

Wanting to know whether the English planned to follow this up with a full scale attack, Charles asked Flinders to glean some information from Mr Hope, then at the island, with the cartel, adding, "oblige moi mon Ami de me les transmettre et elles demeureront ensevelies en moi. Cette connoisance pourroit être très utile aux interêts dont je suis chargé". Charles himself believed that the attack would shortly come. In a letter written on 30th December 1809, Flinders discounted its likelihood: "nobody believes in it here; though it is said that both the English and French officers of the last cartel have declared, that it will not be long delayed. For myself I do not believe the English think either this or your island worth the trouble and expence of attacking and keeping, but they would perhaps be glad to see you neutered". Shortly afterwards, however, when the *Venus* returned with news of yet more prizes, Flinders speculated, "I am mistaken if these repeated captures from the company do not at length draw down an attack upon these islands, which otherwise would not, in my opinion, take place".

After the action on Bourbon, the squadron returned to the Isle of France. On 10th January 1810, Flinders learnt that the Néréide had "chased on shore a Dutch brig from Batavia, last from Bourbon, and set fire to her: I heard her blow up at tea last night". He added "Captain Corbet is more feared here than any other of the cruizers; it is in effect him who has taken most of the vessels here; and in general he appears suddenly, and immediately finds something to do: he appears to be a very active and enterprizing officer". By April rumours were again buzzing of a projected attack upon the Isle of France. Flinders however remained sceptical: "I do not think an attack upon the Isle of France probable". The whispers grew in volume however, when the *Boadicea* and *Magicienne* frigates joined the cruising squadron, and towards the end of May, Decaen was reported to be touring the island's coastal forts. In March 1810, Flinders reiterated his opinion that a British decision to attack would depend on the damage suffered to their trading ships:

I am persuaded, that the question of attack has been an affair of calculation with the Company; and if it finds, that it loses more annually by the French cruizers than the expenses of government and keeping of the island would amount to, then will the Company, from being an opposer become the advocate for taking possession.

Thus within weeks Flinders had changed his opinion, confiding to Charles that he believed Bourbon would be attacked within the year. He added, "the reason which has changed my opinion cannot be very well developed here; and this opinion has no positive information for a basis nor does it immediately extend to the sister island: this is not much, but it is for yourself only". He had evidently been privy to some intelligence, but it was still of a speculative nature.

The next news which Flinders had to impart was based on much firmer information – and was sent from the Cape of Good Hope, to which place he sailed in June 1810, after transferring to the *Otter* from the *Harriet* cartel. He quickly communicated to Charles Desbassayns what he had learned from Colonel Keating: "that there was prospect of your island being almost immediately annexed to the British dominions. I mentioned you to the colonel as being my particular friend, and I trust you will find him to be an useful and agreeable acquaintance".

At the Cape, Admiral Bertie sent for him, and after perusing Flinders' parole, they agreed that "I was under no obligation to refuse any information, that might be required of me relative to that colony and Bourbon" and he answered a number of questions designed to assist the English expeditionary forces who were then making preparations to conquer both the Isles of France and Bourbon. Flinders, however, found the Admiral terse and tetchy, and spent little time with him. He also wrote to Thomi Pitot and to Mme d'Arifat from the Cape sending his letters with English officers heading to those islands. Such was the interest among his confreres to learn about the place he was already calling 'Mauritius', Flinders had dinner invitations almost every evening. He expected that Mme d'Arifat would be visited by officers from the 72nd and 87th regiments, to whom he had sung her praises, and recommended Majors Leitch and Miller to the good offices of Labauve, Thomi Pitot and the Ravel family. Referring to the prospective conquest of the island, as he told Mme d'Arifat, he hoped "que nous serons bientôt compatriotes" and assured her that he had done all he could "pour que cela s'accomplisse sans sang versé. J'ai prêché l'avantage à envoyer une force assez grande pour que les habitants se trouvent dispensés d'une resistance inutile; - je les ai peint comme tolérants, aimables, et généralement bons, tels enfin que je les ai trouvés". When news came in that the conquest of Bourbon – the first of the two islands to be attacked – had been successfully accomplished, Flinders' ship departed for England.

There, on 13 February 1811, hearing a gun salute, he was informed that it was "for the taking of the Isle of France". Two days later he received letters from Pitot and Labauve, which reassured him "all my friends there are well, and some of them satisfied with the change". The first of Thomi's letters, dated 19th September 1810, discussed the taking of Bourbon and the defence preparations being made on his own island. He described Bourbon's capture as:

> cet evenement malheureux pour nous et si déshonorant pour cette isle qui s'est rendue à l'ennemi presque sans aucune resistance. Ce desastre qui semblait devoir nous abattre nous a donné une energie nouvelle et nous a fait prendre la resolution de relever l'honneur du pavillon français humilié dans nos mers par une aussi honteuse capitulation. Nos iles sont aujourd'hui hérissées de batteries plus fortes les unes que les autres. Tous les particuliers sont en armes et du matin au soir s'exercent à tirer à la cible sur de malheureux cipayes de bois qui se trouvent chaque soir criblés de milliers de balles en attendant que leurs redoutables modèles viennent en tâter à leur tour. Nos coups d'essai n'ont pas été malheureux et nos succes ont encore exalté les colons à un point qu'il me serait difficile de vous peindre.

As soon as the capture of Bourbon had been carried out, reported Pitot, the English cruisers had returned to the Isle of France to harass and fatigue the colonists and "de nous fair jetter dans les bras du seduisant Mr Farquhar". He reported that proclamations had been strewn along the coasts, but that "tous les debarquements effectués sur nos côtes ont été repoussés par les habitants de la manière la plus vigoureuse et l'on a vu 250 soldats de ligne fuir en désordre devant 30 ou 40 tirailleurs habitants et abandonner leurs tués sur le champ de bataille". However, he noted that the *Néréide* had been able to surprise the little fort on the Ile de la Passe, which guarded Grand Port in the southeast of the island. He then provided details of a heroic encounter, which terminated in the only defeat of the British navy during the Napoleonic Wars – the battle of Grand Port. On 20th August, at 7 pm, a cousin from that part of the island, informed the family that the French frigates *la Bellone* and *La Minerve* were heading towards Grand Port, where the *Néréide*, commanded by Captain Willoughby was moored, off the Ile de la Passe:

> *A 9 heures un second courier nous a confirmé le rapport du premier et a ajouté que l'isle de la Passe ayant ainsi que la Néréide arboré le pavillon français nos frégates, corvette et une des prises avaient fait route dans le grand port; que la prise le Ceylan avait passé sans reçevoir un coup de canon ni du fort ni de la frégate anglaise, que le Victor qui étant le second avait essuyé le feu des deux ainsi que la Minerve et avaient tous deux perdus quelques hommes, que la Bellone qui était la dernière, avait reviré de bord, s'étant pendant 10 minutes preparée au combat en dehors de l'isle de la Passe et était ensuite entrée resolumment n'avait point répondu au feu du fort, était venue se placer en poupe de la Néréide et l'avait accablé de ses bordées jusqu'à ce que les courants ne l'eussent éloignée et forcée d'aller mouiller avec sa division. Il ne vous sera pas difficile mon ami, connaissant comme vous le faites l'imagination active des français de vous représenter toute notre agitation et le désordre de toutes les têtes. L'ordre est donné de suite aux frégates La Venus, La Manche et l'Astree et à la corvette l'Entreprenant qui se trouvaient désemparés dans le port de se disposer immédiatement à partir. La nuit entière se passa à travailler et*

127

le lendemain à minuit notre division appareilla pour chercher l'ennemi en passant sous le vent.

Les frégates anglaises cependant étaient déjà bien avancées vers leur but - l'une d'elles Le Syrius arriva au Grand Port et mouilla auprès de la Néréide. Les deux autres après avoir lutté deux jours contre les vents parviennent enfin à l'isle de la Passe et le soir même tous les 4 appareillent sous leurs focs et viennent attaquer notre division bien preparée à les reçevoir.

Aussitôt que l'ennemi fut approché suffisamment de nos frégates pour en être atteint leur feu commença sans quil daignent répondre un seul coup avançant toujours la Néréide en tête. La lenteur imposante avec laquelle les anglais avançaient, leur silence lugubre avaient je ne sais quoi d'effrayant, de sinistre qui resserrait tous les coeurs excepté ceux de nos braves marins.

Mais près d'arriver le Syrius touche sur un paté de corail il est a portée de canon mais ne peut faire usage que de 5 ou 6 canons. La Magicienne et l'Iphigenie touchent aussi quelque tems après mais sur la vase et parviennent à s'embosser de manière à offrir le travers à nos frégates. La Néréide mouille à demi portée de fusil de la Bellone et le feu aussitôt devient général.

La déstruction de l'une des deux divisions devient le seul moyen de salut qui reste à l'autre et tout ce que l'acharnement le plus obstiné, la rage la plus terrible peut faire est employé de part et d'autre pour écraser l'ennemi. L'adresse des manoeuvres n'est plus pour rien dans cette affaire le courage seul doit décider et après 2 heures de combat la Néréide amène son pavillon; mais l'obscurité est si grande, le bruit si terrible que la Bellone n'en peut être informée et son terrible feu continue sur la malheureuse Néréide. A minuit cependant un des 18 français pris sur l'isle de la Passe n'entendant plus tirer la Néréide brisa ses fers, monte sur le pont de cette frégate et vient à la nage prevenir la terre que la Néréide est amenée. Mais le Syrius ouvre son feu sur cette malheureuse frégate et empêche qu'on ne puisse l'amariner jusqu'au lendemain matin.

A detail from the Battle of Grand Port

French and British participants in the battle:
Duperré and Willoughby

A 9 heures et demi les amarres de la Minerve sont coupées et elle vient s'echouer sur la vase mais assez heureusement pour que son feu n'en soit ni gené ni rallenti. Peu d'instants après la Bellone éprouve le même accident et le même bonheur. Le Ceylon continue aussi le combat avec vigueur. Mr Duperré Capitaine de la Bellone est blessé vers 10 heures d'un biscayen à la joue; un de ses officiers le croit mort et veut en dérober la connaissance à l'equipage. Il l'enlève dans ses bras mais est renversé avec lui dans la calle. On emporte à terre le brave Duperré sans connaissance. ... nos braves marins redoublent de courage et de fureur à même que leur danger s'accroit. Le Capitaine Bouvet établit un pont entre les deux frégates et les commande à la fois. Au point du jour la Néréide parait dans l'etat le plus terrible et portant pavillon français arboré par les prisonniers de l'isle de la Passe. Un équipage français va à bord et trouve cent morts dans le pont et 70 blessés. Le Capitaine Willoughby lui même renversé et nageant dans son sang sans secours est transporté à terre et y reçoit tous les soins nécessaires. La Magicienne desemparée criblée de coups de canon est devenue à son tour la point de mire de tous les vaisseaux et les anglais incapables d'en supporter la furie l'abondonnent et y mettent le feu. Le tour du Syrius comme son feu a cessé et il s'empresse à retenir son equipage qu'il transporte sur l'Iphigenie et le fort de la Passe.

Lambert jette à la mer ses rechanges, une partie de ses canons et réussit enfin à se relever et à se tirer de dessous nos bordées qui pendant quelques heures avaient à peine discontinué quelques moments pour raffraichir les équipages.

Cependant la division de la Venus affalée sous le vent par les courants et les vents continues, faisant d'inutiles efforts pour arriver à la tête de l'isle; nos montagnes ne l'apperçoivent plus et l'on ne sait ce qu'elle est devenue. Elle reparait enfin mais devant le port Napoleon et escortant un vaisseau de 400 tonneaux chargé de munitions de guerre et de bouche qu'elle a capturé dans le canal; elle remonte cette fois par le vent et arrive au Grand Port 24 heures après la cessation du combat. Les anglais en la voyant sentent l'impossibilité d'échapper et se rendent à discretion.

Flinders wrote to an acquaintance in Cape Town that he had learnt of the "sad work at the Isle of France".

Before long, however, it was Pitot who was expressing his "vive douleur" in a letter dated 7th December 1810, and which recounted the return of the English in force to conquer the Isle of France – which would henceforth be known as Mauritius. Pitot volunteered a number of reasons for the disarray of his compatriots in the face of the enemy. The Isle of France, he stated, was without help from the home government, penniless, and short of supplies at the moment of the attack. The inhabitants were consequently discouraged and the navy disunited, while the counter-offensive had been thrown into disorder by the news that the slaves were taking advantage of the soldiers' absence to pillage their properties and by the ill-advised decision to distribute a portion of the troops' overdue pay on the day the enemy disembarked and which had occasioned an outbreak of drunkenness. Finally, according to Pitot, the necessity to man the large number of coastal fortifications had divided the forces and significantly reduced the numbers available to repel the enemy troops advancing on the town. He described the events surrounding the conquest and his own dramatic involvement, as follows:

> une force considérable expediée de toutes les parties de l'Inde nous a attaqués et puis presque sans résistance une capitulation honorable pour le militaire mais ruineuse pour le commerce nous a été accordée et maintenant notre ville est pleine de figures nouvelles dont nous n'avons cependant pas encore eu lieu de nous plaindre. Notre port est aussi rempli des batiments anglais qui nous ont versé ce deluge d'hommes. Ce coup … a pourtant cela de consolant qu'il prouve que l'ennemi a su nous estimer et qu'il a beaucoup trop fait pour la resistance que nous étions en etat de lui opposer. Vous reconnaitrez à ce langage mon cher ami, votre ancien disputeur en politique. Celui dont le coeur a toujours été ouvert au particulier malheureux de votre pays, mais que les torts et l'oubli de sa mère patrie n'ont pu dégouté du nom français. Aussi mon ami, n'ai je pu me décider à vous rendre la colonie sans faire au moins le coup de feu avec nos vainqueurs.

J'étais avec mon frère Edouard et Frederic Pitot au nombre de ceux que le général a envoyé au devant de l'ennemi. Notre petite colonne d'environ 300 hommes, dont cent de garde nationale a attaqué resolument l'ennemi sur le chemin du tombeau et le feu de deux pièces de campagne a jetté un moment le désordre dans la première colonne ennemie. Ce désordre a duré toutes fois que quelques secondes et après 10 ou 15 minutes de fusillade notre petit corps a été obligé de fuir en désordre sous le feu de 8 à 10 mille ennemis qui nous criblaient de balles. Ayant perdu mon frère de vue je me suis dirigé entre les montagnes de Pitheboth et du Pouce et j'ai passé a Moka d'où j'ai ecrit au Port pour savoir si Edouard y était rendu. On m'a répondu que non. ...
Alors mon ami le desespoir s'est emparé de moi. J'ai erré de habitation en habitation pour avoir quelques renseignements et nulle part je n'en ai pu reçevoir. Je sus arrivé trois jours après le combat à la Poudre d'Or écrasé de fatigue, brulé du soleil, mourant de faim et de soif et de plus la mort dans le coeur. Rendu à la plus voisine habitation de M Rouillard j'ai questionné et j'ai su qu'on ne savait rien encore de mon pauvre frère alors je n'ai plus eu d'esperance de le trouver que parmi les blessés ou les prisonniers et j'allais m'acheminer vers le camp anglais lorsqu'un noir m'a annoncé qu'Edouard au moment de la déroute renversé par les fuyards, foulé aux pieds, meurtri, sans connaissance avait été relevé par l'ennemi mais bientôt abandonné par eux et rejetté à terre. Il est resté à terre sous le feu du soleil et presque sans connaissance depuis 7 ou 8 heures du matin jusqu'au soir ou le fraicheur l'a un peu ranimé et lui a permis de se remettre entre les mains de l'ennemi qui l'a traité avec humanité. Il nous a enfin été rendu lors de la capitulation.

Mme d'Arifat's version of the momentous changes that had taken place was delivered with her usual equanimity. Her letter to Flinders, informed him: "c'est votre pavillon qui flotte partout en cette isle. Ce grand evenement s'est accompli sans que nous ayons une seule larme à repandre - nos parens, amis, tous sont sains et saufs". Like Pitot she pronounced the capitulation "très honorable, très favorable aux habitans".

Over the following months, the letters sent from the islands began to focus on life under the English administration, both in terms of opportunities, and setbacks. In January 1811, Thomi Pitot expressed the fear that "the most considerable and respectable part of this colony" would be obliged to sacrifice their fortunes and attachments and leave "a country where their conscience is hurt by a requested oath of obedience, submission and fidelity to the English Government". Ultimately, most of the colonists would sign the oath, - a copy of which is still extant in the Mauritius Archives – but Pitot railed against an order that obliged the French colonists

> to break for the present every ties between us and our mother country, exposes ourselves to the vengeance of the emperor, ruins all those who have properties in France, deprives them of all their rights of inheriting these, even of their own father, or obliges them to lose the half of their fortune to take away the other part and for the last stroke leaves not to us even this restriction so natural that we will not take arms in case of an attack against our brethren and countrymen.

Pitot, for his own part, was obliged to remain, on account of his family ties, and whilst pledging quiet obedience to the laws of England, stated that he considered himself, "a vanquished enemy, never as a subject of your King. You have been a prisoner in our country I will be the same now". At the same time he acknowledged that Farquhar's administration seemed destined to be "soft and advantageous to the private inhabitants", while Mr Abercromby was considered as "our saviour for having agreed to the proposals of General Decaen and prevented the excesses which the soldiers were disposed to commit in the town and the country houses".

While the colonists were anxiously weighing up the pros and cons of their change of government, in India - as Hope reported to Flinders - the merchants were rejoicing that the 'nest of privateers' had finally been extinguished: "it is incredible the satisfaction which the capture of that Island has diffused all over India". And now the ex-POWs, Flinders included, began to consider the advantages that they could hope to expect from their involvement in the victorious expedition. Hope was quickly recompensed. In February 1811, he wrote from Calcutta: "I am now on the way for Batavia where I am to accompany Lord Minto. You may judge from that the satisfaction which my mission to the Isle of France has given".

Captain W.F. Owen, who had left with Flinders, travelling to India on the *Harriet*, had also been "much questioned relative to the Isle of France" and had "not failed to endeavor to set them in the right way". He drafted a memorandum, "adverting to the politics which should govern us in an attack and giving such military and local hints as I considered necessary to securing the conquest". Owen's memorandum was drawn up, he said "on the principle of saving blood and ill blood", a principle that he knew Flinders would admire, and to it he attributed the decision to attack Mauritius with a force "little short of 20 thousand". Flinders too, believed that he had played his part in the successful preparation of the expedition. Writing to Commodore Rowley, in February 1811, he stated, "I know not whether the sketch of the port and town of Port Louis, and the information upon the finances and strength of the island, and the dispositions of the inhabitants, which I gave to admiral Bertie at the Cape, were of any advantage in making the dispositions, and in the attack; but I believe that everything proved to be as I had pointed out". And he and Owen were not alone in laying their claims. There was political advantage and economic gain to be had from the recognition of services rendered.

While Flinders' claims in England were barely listened to, his friends were faring better in the newest of the English colonies. Chazal was an old friend of Farquhar's and derived considerable benefit from his ties with the Governor of Mauritius, while in Bourbon, Charles Desbassayns accepted the post of Inspector General under the new British administration. According to Mme d'Arifat, then visiting the Desbassayns, to anyone with "une parfaite connaissance du caractère et des gouts de Charles" this was indeed a sacrifice in the public interest. In the event, he only remained in the post for three months.

Flinders meanwhile, now found himself in the position of acting as advisor and seeking to allay the fears of those who had formerly performed similar services for him. The colonists, anxious about the future of the islands under English hands, wrote to him for reassurance. Responding to Mr Curtat in June 1811, Flinders expressed his opinion of the Governor Farquhar, and the likelihood of a replacement being sent out:

> The goodness of his character is generally allowed, but that is not everything required in a governor. The ministers look for firmness, probably to resist indiscrete importunity, ability to execute their orders, and to distinguish character, and economy in the administration of the finances. Now it does not appear that this last quality, makes one of the many possessed by Mr. F.; and I should not be surprised if some officer, or nobleman, unaccustomed to the Indian manner of administrating, was soon to be sent out.

To Thomi Pitot, Flinders offered his views on the future of commerce there: "I do not know anything that you could send advantageously to England, unless perhaps, cotton. Coffee and sugar are quite a drug; but when you hear that any considerable number of the ports on the continent are open, you may then send coffee". By July 1812, he reported:

> with respect to the commerce of your island, I fear nothing is yet settled; nor perhaps will it until the affair of the Company's charter is decided, which will be in less than two years. There is little doubt that you will then have a free commerce with England, as well as with India. To be advantageous to you, however, the markets of the continent must be opened, either wholly or in part; and this the French emperor still opposes with the most determined perseverance: He is now upon the confines of Russia, and what will be the result, Heaven alone knows.

The English government of the islands brought changes in the administration, many posts in which had been occupied by the French inhabitants. Pitot reported that their friend, Antoine Bayard, had lost his place as a judge, having been found to be deaf, but Mme d'Arifat offered the more cheerful news that Colonel Keating had promised a post in Bourbon to her son

Aristide. However, as the British brought their own protégés to the island from India, the colonists increasingly found that they were dismissed from their posts. Mme d'Arifat informed Flinders in January 1812 that "mon fils Aristide ainsi qu'une infinité d'autres a perdu son petit emploi ... peu à peu les français ont été éloignés des emplois, pour les donner aux anglois, et les emplois subalternes sont donnés aux malabards". The cartels returning to France were filled with colonists, and the Sauveget family was among those planning to leave.

Soon Flinders began to hear complaints that the English government of the islands was performing badly. To Mr Pitot, he wrote: "I am truly sorry to hear of the state of public affairs in Mauritius; and the nonsensical stories by which the peace of the colony is disturbed. You will, by degrees, have a new set of officers and probably a new governor; and I do most sincerely hope, that you will be more happy and prosperous". And to the Port Louis based lawyer, Antoine Curtat, he stated:

> It gives me great pain to learn from all hands, that the inhabitants of the islands are so much less happy than I had hoped they would be under the British dominion. Mr. Farquhar himself seems to be esteemed; but those under him, it is to be hoped, will be very soon displaced by appointments from England. In little more than a year, the charter of the East India Company will undergo a modification; by which the commerce of your colonies are likely to be gainers; and I think there is great reason to hope that your situation will speedily improve in every respect.

However, even those families, like the Desbassayns, who had been so helpful to the English in Bourbon, found that the British government was not prepared to assist them with their property affairs on the islands. The colonial department in London was flooded with petitions from French landed proprietors in the colonies who wished to return to their island homes, or to make arrangements to dispose of their investments. A deaf ear was turned to most of these pleas. In a letter to Mme d'Arifat, Flinders informed her that

136

Panon Desbassayns and his good wife still remain our neighbours; but it is uncertain how long the government will suffer them to live in England. They unfortunately came direct from France; and Philip, who has been much amongst our great people, has caused some suspicions to be entertained of his motives; and these have done no service to Panon. Their affairs are perfectly unconnected; but it is not easy to convince the government of it.

Flinders sought to help the Desbassayns, addressing a number of letters to the British government in which he acknowledged his links with the family and stressed the role they had played, in offering hospitality to the English officers at the time of their island's conquest. Mme Debsassayns the elder, he said, had received the officers of two Indiamen, taken to Bourbon, at her home, while Commodore Rowley and Colonel Keating

considered themselves under great obligations to the family of Desbassayns, for the services and kindness which they, and those under their command, received at their hands, both at, and after the taking of Bourbon by our forces. On the Commodore's return to the bay of St Paul's, after an action with French frigates, when there was no hospital for the sick and wounded, Mme Desbassayns received and took care of them.

This fact, he stated, had been sufficient to convince the government to permit the return home of Henry Desbassayns. He also mentioned that Mr Philip Desbassayns, had shown "many kindnesses to Englishmen in France", and acknowledged his indebtedness to him for "the friendly zeal with which he aided the application of the Admiralty to obtain justice for me from the French government". Had it not been for his exertions, Flinders contended, "it is presumable that my liberation from the parole under which I was improperly placed by Gen De Caen, would not have been obtained".

The French government proved little more sympathetic to the Mauritian Creoles. In July 1812, Flinders reported to Mme d'Arifat that those inhabitants of Bourbon and Mauritius who refused to take the oath of allegiance and went to France, were *sadly disappointed in their expectations. Instead of being caressed for their fidelity, and obtaining situations equal to what they had given up, Buonaparte, when applied to in their favour, answered "I should like to see anybody refuse me the oath of allegiance, in any country I conquer"! And there are very few of those persons who are not seeking for opportunities to return. Pray tell Mr. Sauvejet this, and recommend to weigh everything well before he quits his little retreat at the Rivière des Lataniers.*

Charles Desbassayns was taking a more long-term view. In November 1812, he asked Flinders' opinion on the fate of the islands: "do you suppose in the event of a temporary peace that they are likely to be returned to their former owner?" He wondered, however, whether England could so soon forget the damage occasioned to her commerce. Flinders offered the following speculations in his reply:

What may be the fate of your colonies, in the event of a peace, can be only conjectured. Our minister, as well as the E.I. Company, are well aware of the consequences of giving them back to France; yet circumstances may be such, at the making of peace as to render this inevitable. ... It is a grievous thing to hear on all hands of the state of the government in your islands; and it is particularly so to me, who am interested in them, and hoped the colonists would be so much more happy under the English than the French dominion. By degrees, however, as the officers of the government will be replaced by others from England, I trust better times will arise, and happiness and prosperity ensue.

Desbassayns also shared the general disappointment in the men sent by Britain to govern their new acquisitions:

they have neither talents, judgment, nor justice, they trample all our laws at their will and even their own laws they are ignorant of. When the French laws are useful to their purpose they are called to their aid, and plead the capitulation, when they may protect any one from any injustice or arbitrary act they are totally laid by. Your own countrymen blush at their conduct, and such spirit of intrigues I never saw before.

138

While Bourbon was indeed to be handed back to the French in 1814, Mauritius remained very much a backwater of the vast British Empire, with a colonial staff composed of men who needed to be 'placed', rather than men destined for greatness.

At least the unseating of Napoleon gave Flinders an opportunity to rejoice, with Charles: "the tyrant is fallen, never to rise again. France is once more herself again, and when the revolutionary principles shall be purged off, she will be as she ought, an object of pride and ornament to Europe. All is peace, joy and exultation, and Europe entire is in a delirium of joy". Charles Baudin, writing from Toulon in June 1814, attributed to these events, a lesson for all:

> *La France est abaissée; l'Angleterre est à l'apogée de son bonheur: puissent vos compatriotes apprendre par le terrible exemple qui vient d'être donné à l'univers, combien peu est stable la puissance fondée sur l'injustice et exercée par l'orgueil.*

Unfortunately, as Flinders noted, "I suffer too much to be able to express my feelings at any length". The long-looked for peace, and the much-anticipated completion of his *Voyage to Terra Australis*, had come too late.

Napoleon – the vanquished enemy

A British prison ship, or pontoon,
aboard which many French POWs were held.

The support network

In August 1804 Flinders first began to realize that the French inhabitants of Mauritius were going out of their way to offer him support, both moral and material. On learning that a group of the capital's residents had determined to represent his case to the local authorities, he speculated: "a natural sense of justice seems to be the leading feature in this transaction of theirs, but I believe also that they fear to draw down the resentment of the British government upon their island". He had astutely recognized that the colonists' overtures of friendship to himself and other POWs were motivated both by sympathy for their plight, and by an insular instinct of self-preservation. Despite their continuing attachment to France, the colonists had no desire blindly to follow the excesses of Revolution. For some years prior to Flinders' arrival, their elected assembly had stood in open revolt to the diktat of France and the islanders had run their own affairs. The sending of Napoleon's emissary, General Decaen, was intended both to placate and to subdue them, but they remained sceptical of French policy, only too aware that their very survival depended on delicate handling of the representatives of those nations who traded with them, and of those who threatened them.

1. A tireless referee

Thus it was, that Flinders was very soon being called upon to issue letters of recommendation to colonists of his acquaintance who were venturing beyond the confines of the island. While still in the Maison Despeaux at Port Louis, he penned missives in favour of M. Quenot – a friend of Captain Bergeret, and Messrs Joseph and Edward Merle – relatives of the Pitot family. In May 1805, he was gratified to learn that the Merles had arrived back on the island from Madras. Flinders noted, "they do not know how it was that they were selected to receive this indulgence, but think it must have been in consequence of the letter which I wrote about 5 months since to Lord Bentinck, the governor of Madras, concerning them". This was confirmed by Mr Baudin, and Flinders later wrote to his friend, Captain Henry of the 19th regiment of dragoons in India, to pass on his thanks to Bentinck.

In December, again at the request of Thomi, Flinders prepared a letter for Monsieur Gravier, a surgeon and a member of the literary societies of the island, addressed "to the commander of any of His Majestys ships in India", and requesting that if taken, Mr Gravier be released immediately on parole, or be offered "the most liberal treatment and earliest exchange" which could be granted. A similar letter was written for Mr Deglos, who was also planning a voyage to India, around the same time. In the course of 1806, again at the behest of Pitot, letters for Leguen and Boisgris were despatched. For his own friend, Charles Baudin, Flinders drafted a particularly warm letter of recommendation on 15th May 1806:

> *The established character of the commanders of His Majestys ships for their liberal treatment of those whom the chance of war throws into their hands, might render unnecessary the recommendation of any particular individual to their notice and protection; but I cannot dispense myself from saying something of Mr. Charles Baudin, an enterprising young officer, who will present this to you. The acknowledgements I owe him for the zealous efforts he has made by means of his friends of the Institute of Paris to relieve me from an imprisonment in this Island, as unjust as it is unparalleled, render this an indispensable act of Justice. Mr. Baudin made the voyage of discovery in the Géographe, and though very young gained to himself reputation by his talents and spirit of enterprise; and learned to appreciate the labours of those employed in the cause of science and humanity, to whatever nation they might belong. Persuaded that his understanding and manners will amply indemnify you for the attention you may be pleased to shew him, in the pleasure you will receive from his conversation and acquaintance, I doubt not you will pleased that I have pointed him out to you.*

When Pitot himself also planned a trip – to Bourbon - Flinders drafted a special letter for him on 22nd July 1806 requesting that he "might be supplied with money for bills which authorized him to draw upon my agent, along with the usual letter for the commander of the British ship which might take him prisoner". Pitot was described as a "respectable merchant...whose character is equally estimable for his literary qualifications, and virtues of his heart, of which others of our countrymen, prisoners in this island, have reaped the advantage".

As word spread, other colonists began to approach Flinders with requests for such laissez-passers for their friends. M. Palerne, for example, arrived at Le Refuge one day in August 1806, bearing a letter from a Mr A. McDonald, a former POW on the Isle of France, addressed to Jacques Michel Menesse. From this Flinders learnt that Menesse, formerly an inhabitant of the French settlement of Mahé in India, and an officer in the Pondicherry regiment, "had done many little kindnesses to several English prisoners". Menesse needed to return to India on account of his father's death. Flinders accordingly wrote out a letter in favour of that gentleman.

In September, Jacques Mallac, another of Pitot's friends, was also the subject of a similar letter, in which he was recommended to Englishmen as "a member of the Society of Emulation and one of the pleasantest men in the Isle of France". Mallac was journeying to Bourbon to attend a marriage, "to which I am sure his presence will be a vast accession of gaiety", wrote Flinders. Adopting a lightheartedness of tone, uncommon in these missives, he requested, should Mallac's ship be taken, that he be

> put ashore if possible at Bourbon before the celebration of the ceremony which is the cause of his voyage; for although he may not be able, physically, to turn water into wine as was once done upon a similar occasion, he is well able to do it morally, by the inebriation which the sallies of his wit do not fail to produce even upon water drinkers.

Evidently Mr Mallac had made a strong impression on Flinders.

Soon, Flinders was even being accosted in the street, for the favour that his pen could supply. Mme Murville met him on the road, in November 1806, and begged for a letter recommending her brother-in-law, Mr Robert, who was planning a journey to Calcutta. In December, De Glos and Gravier were again given letters for a second voyage they were undertaking, and Frederic Pitot, Thomi's cousin, who proposed to go to Batavia, made a third.   In January 1807, Thomi requested a letter of recommendation for Germinil Chauvet, whom Flinders described as "the son of a Bourbon family with whom he is particularly united". In March, Labat, a French-Mauritian prisoner in India was also accorded the benefit of Flinder's letter-writing skills, and in April, Charles Desbassayns, was recommended in the strongest manner, as a gentleman to whom "I have obligations for his polite attention to me in my confinement". M. de Mouhy, a relation of the d'Arifats, who was leaving on a voyage to Madagascar, was accorded the same favour as his compatriots.

These arrangements were evidently reciprocal, insofar as this was possible, for while Thomi Pitot was in Bourbon on one of his business trips, he informed Flinders that he had been able to intercede with the authorities there in favour of one Captain Davidson, 'a meritorious and good man', to enable him to sail for Mauritius. There were also personal arrangements made, as when the Swiss merchant, Johann Boand, who had been so helpful to Flinders, proposed to make a voyage to Asia and Flinders wrote a private letter to his friend, the botanist Christopher Smith, on Boand's behalf.

The d'Arifat family also had occasion to be grateful to the English: in mid 1805 Labauve was taken prisoner by the *Pitt*, in sight of Bourbon, "but spoke handsomely of his treatment from Captain Vashon". Flinders knew Vashon and reminded him of the incident: "you may perhaps remember [Labauve] from the circumstance of his offering you the bayonet of his musquet, but that instead of taking it you returned him his musquet and his black servant also".

By now, however, the sheer volume of correspondence which Flinders was generating had begun to alarm him. Thus, when Boand requested him to make another application to Lord Bentinck in favour of a young French prisoner there, named Pierre Marie Guezenec, Flinders hesitated. He wrote instead to his friend Major Henry stating, "I know not how my lord might consider a third application of this sort from me, and am therefore afraid to make it. You see my lord sometimes, and perhaps your representation might have the desired effect, and would oblige me very much". Flinders also wrote to Thomi Pitot explaining that he could no longer offer such recommendations, unless he knew of "some services rendered to English prisoners, or some extraordinary merit" which he could cite. This communication had been occasioned by Pitot's request for letters on behalf of Messrs. Malherbe and Martin Bedier, but as Flinders warned, "you will agree that some caution is requisite, and I am sure you do not desire me to injure my own reputation by acting a part unbecoming a British commander".

An alternative mark of attention was to introduce French Mauritians to English gentlemen of Flinder's acquaintance. Thus, in May 1807, he addressed a letter to former POW Walter Robertson, to present Monsieur Laroche Souvestre:

> *the son in law of Monsieur Foisy, president of the Society of Emulation, who is about to embark for India with the intention of fixing himself there. The situation of Mr. Foisy will shew you the consideration he enjoys in this island, and I have to add that I have myself received marks of attention from him, and know that he has been useful to Lieut. McCartney of the native cavalry when a prisoner, and I believe to others. I have not the pleasure of being personally acquainted with Monsieur Souvestre, but am assured that he is a worthy young man, and … I am sure I need say no more to induce you to give him a favourable reception, and facilitate his introduction into Society.*

Notwithstanding his concerns, Flinders' good heart made it difficult for him to refuse the requests of his friends. He wrote a recommendation for Mallac's son, travelling from France, and another for Barthelemy's son, Felix Froberville, returning from

Batavia. He relented in favour of Mr Guezenec, addressing a letter on his behalf to Sir Edward Pellew, and when Chevreau asked for a letter of introduction for Mr Gourel de St Pern, the cousin of his wife, once again, Flinders complied.

In October 1808, with the departure of a ship to France, numerous applications being made to him, Flinders had to be selective. He had much good to say of Captain Motard, and to help Francis Malherbe, an acquaintance of the d'Arifats, who was taking his son to be educated in England, he proposed to "write a few lines to Mr. Park, master attendant in Portsmouth yard". In April 1809, he declined to offer a further letter to Mr Laroche Souvestre, who already had recommendations obtained from Lieutenant Owen, and Captain Woolcombe. Flinders did not approve of the letters those officers had given him, complaining that they were "written in a bombastic style, boasting of the superiority of English over Frenchmen, and abusing the French government and its adherents; and in my opinion highly improper to be borne by a French subject whatever may be his private sentiments".

When Mr Garnier, a painter who had travelled with Nicolas Baudin, happened to ask for a letter of recommendation, it gave Flinders an opportunity to contrast his treatment with that accorded to the French explorer. However, as he told Garnier, he could not consider him as part of that expedition:

> vous avez quitté l'expedition avant qu'elle soit rendue à la terre qui en était l'objet; - vous ne vous êtes pas rejoint à elle à l'epoque de son retour à l'Isle de France; - vos ouvrages, tout estimable que je ne doute pas qu'ils soient, ne sont pas faits ni dans l'expédition ni dans le pays de ses recherches.

Garnier's reaction to this dismissive letter is unknown, but there were always more people who had reason to be grateful for Flinder's help, than individuals who were refused.

In October 1809, for example, he was pleased to receive a letter of thanks from Mr Quenot – "it appears that the recommendation I had given him when I was in the Maison

Despeaux had been very serviceable to him during the six months he had been prisoner at the Cape and on board the cruizers". And when the colonists really were taken – as happened to the Desbassayns brothers, travelling from America – Flinders took further steps to enquire after them. On this occasion, he addressed a letter in their behalf to his patron, Sir Joseph Banks, in February 1809. He later received a letter of thanks from Panon Desbassayns, "from which I conclude my letter had been useful to him during his captivity in England".

Hugh Hope, in India, also did what he could for those colonists considered to be the friends of Englishmen. In January 1811 he told Flinders, "upon the departure of the expedition from this place I gave letters to some of the principal officers to our friends the Pitots and Kerbalanecs, to secure to their families every possible protection". When a cartel carrying French prisoners arrived in India with 'young Kerbalanec' on board, Hope reported "I have shewn Kerbalanec every attention in my favour…[he has] been received everywhere with the greatest kindness which is rather an extraordinary thing for John Bull".

2. Lobbyist for french prisoners

Flinders' attempts to help the French Creole prisoners of war was becoming a major occupation, and this would continue and increase following his return to England. The considerable efforts he made for Edouard Ossère, a nephew of Mme Curtat, kept a prisoner aboard a hulk at Plymouth since the taking of the *Marengo*, are a case in point. While still at the Isle of France he addressed a letter to the Transport Board in the young man's behalf. A few months' later, back in England, Flinders wrote to Ossère himself, wishing to deal with his financial and other problems. By November 1810, he had managed to extricate him from the prison ship on which he had been held for 5 long years, gave him £10 to purchase clothes, and arranged with bankers at Odiham for the monthly payment of £2 to be given to Ossère.

147

He visited the prisoners – Chamisso, Kerbalanec, Gourel de St Pern, and Ossère - in Hampshire with his brother, to provide them with the money and letters which their relatives had entrusted to him. They were not effusive with their thanks, however, and Flinders felt that they had not expected him to make the journey. This discouraged him somewhat from making further visits to the prison ships, but he continued to be active on their behalf from London. He passed on family and political news, for example, to a despondent Edward Merle, a prisoner at Moreton Hampstead, in November 1810, and sought also to extricate M. Baudouin from the *Suffolk* prison ship at Portsmouth, from where he was sent to Peebles in Scotland, in company with Renault de St. Germain. Flinders tried to explain to the anxious young men why their liberation – dependent on the arrival of French cartels – was delayed, and to encourage them with his kind words and unfailing attentions. He recommended that they write to their families on Mauritius, to ask for the governor's support, since the liberation of prisoners was facilitated by representations made to Farquhar.

In February 1811 he addressed a request to the Admiralty Office for the release of the young men. He described Salaun de Kerbalanec as the nephew of "one of the richest merchants in the island and the friend of English prisoners in general", and Gourel de St Pern as being related to "many respectable families in both islands from some of whom I received many marks of friendship during my long imprisonment in the Isle of France". Edouard Ossère was recommended as the nephew of Curtat - "a principal man of the law at Port Louis, to whom I was under many obligations", Edouard Merle, as a relation of his friend Pitot and M. Céré - son of the late superintendant of the botanical garden - was described as "brother of M Laurent Barbé a respectable planter and to Madame Bedar, who so kindly received two English ladies into her house, when taken in the *Windham*, going to Bengal". Kerbalanec and Céré had served on the *Belle Poule*, while Ossère and St Pern, were from the *Marengo*.

Flinders was informed in response that the Earl of Liverpool, was "of opinion that much circumspection should be observed in permitting persons of this description to proceed to the Isles of France and Bourbon", and that it was not "expedient under the present circumstances to issue directions for the release of these prisoners". After much correspondence, however, the Transport Board finally directed the release of the five men, in June 1811, and Flinders sent off another round of letters, to each of the young men, and to their relatives at the Isle of France. The duties had been wearisome – he told Pitot that "poor Merle has been very impatient, and not always very considerate" and much of the money advanced to Ossère had come out of his own pocket, but he was pleased to have been able to make some repayment for the many kindnesses shown him in Mauritius.

Of course, this set in train the same cycle of obligations which had occurred with the references he had been accustomed to write while in the Isle of France. No sooner had the efficacy of his intervention been shown, than he began to receive requests for help from other French prisoners in England. Joseph Ribet wrote to him on 25th June 1811, from Devon, and M. Ducasse, who was on board the *Veteran* prison ship in Portsmouth Harbour, applied for Flinders' help in July. To Felix Roger, aboard the prison ship *Crown Prince* at Chatham, Flinders wrote, as to the others "il me peine de savoir qu'il y ait encore un autre créole de l'Isle de France prisonnier ici; et surtout en ce qu'il est hors de mon pouvoir de leur être utile dans ce moment".

He nevertheless began again with his trips to the Transport and Admiralty offices to enquire about these prisoners and meanwhile tried to encourage them to make use of the most effective channels to ensure their release. To Mr de Boucherville, also on board the *Crown* prison ship in Portsmouth, he explained:

> The creoles of the islands are not likely to be released, except in the case that the English governor shall apply for them to the Transport Board, or to the Secretary of State... I would therefore recommend to you to write to your friends, and request them to apply to the English governor for your return.

In September 1811, Flinders wrote to Admiral Sir Roger Curtis, at Portsmouth, on behalf of further Isle of France prisoners, in particular Mme Brunet, Thomi Pitot's sister, who had been aboard a cartel brought to England as a prize. She had written to Flinders, complaining of the conditions of their captivity. "I perhaps owe my life to the humanity and kind attention of many of the principal inhabitants of that island", he wrote to the Admiral - in vain, for months went past, without any respite for Mme Brunet. In December, he wrote to Thomi, deprecating

> how much she has had to suffer; on board the Wellesley, from the unhandsome treatment of the captor; and on board the Orlando from the perverseness of the winds and the rigour of our climate. Poor woman I sincerely pitied her; and am not at all surprised that everything she has suffered from different causes, should be charged to the injustice and cruelty of the whole English nation.

Flinders was happy to be able to write to Mme d'Arifat, soon afterwards, that Mme Brunet and the other passengers from the Wellesley had sailed for Morlaix, and that their case, having been decided in the Court of Amiralty, "the money and merchandise have been ordered to be restored to the French owners: a decision which gives me infinite pleasure; first because it is just, and next because my friends are concerned in it".

He also had the satisfaction to receive a letter from Mme d'Arifat, dated 14 January 1812, in which she stated that Ossère had spent a few days with the family and was full of gratitude for what Flinders had done for him. She added that the Chevreau family were also much obliged to him on behalf of their cousin St Pern, "enfin mon cher Monsieur, la manière dont vous vous êtes comporté envers ces pauvres prisonniers attire sur vous bien des bénédictions". Mme d'Arifat also informed Flinders that a M. Rondineau had written to her, asking for assistance in favour of his son, who was held at Dartmoor, and had been a prisoner for 7 years. She sent Ossère to him instead, to explain the procedures, remarking that if she had acceded to his request for a letter to Flinders, many others would have followed, and he would have been overwhelmed. In fact, M. Rondineau had found another means of reaching Flinders, who received a letter from him in August 1812, but as Mme d'Arifat had anticipated he was unable to offer much hope to the anxious father:

> *I am sorry to say that there are, at this time, seven or eight other creoles whom I either know personally or am acquainted with their families, and whom I have been seeking opportunities to serve for these twelve months past, but in vain; and that I am receiving applications from different parts of England and Scotland asking for that assistance and interest.*

To Madame d'Arifat herself, Flinders wrote: "I am sorry it has not been in my power to do anything useful either for young Boucherville or Rondineau. I have no influence whatever with the government".

Flinders meanwhile continued to follow up the cases of those prisoners from families he had frequented on the Isle of France. In 1812, he again addressed Robert Peel on the subject of M. de Boucherville, then held at Forton, and wrote a letter to the superintendant of the Alien Office, seeking permission for M. Favier and Mme Monneron to proceed to the Isle of France. Again, Lord Liverpool refused his request, on the grounds that "no person coming from France, or from countries under the control of France, [are] permitted to go out to the colonies". Later that year, Flinders wrote to Thomi "I have done everything in my power both for Mad. Monneron and M. Favier; but unfortunately, that everything has not been much". Mme Monneron was staying at Blackheath, where Flinders visited her in November 1812, while Favier had arrived bearing a letter of introduction from Captain Bergeret in Morlaix.

On 11 May, in a separate letter to Pitot, Flinders reported that "young Boucherville and some other creoles are still prisoners here, nor can I do anything to obtain their release". He repeated that only the favour of the governor, Farquhar, could procure this. He noted that Boucherville was confined on a prison ship, "having been foolish enough not to keep his parole with strictness". A few days later, on a visit to Portsmouth, he paid a visit to Mr Boucherville on board the *Veteran*. He also contacted

Farquhar's brother at Boucherville's request, but was informed that the governor had received no petition from the family. The letters appealing for help written by Messrs Joseph Merven, another parole breaker, and Maingard, "gave me pain", as Flinders told them: "feeling on the one side a strong desire to serve a creole of the Isle of France, and especially a friend of Mr. Pitot; and knowing that, on the other, I had exhausted every interest I could make with the Admiralty and Transport Office". Désiré Geffroy, taken in the *Belle Poule* was another unfortunate 'parole breaker'. Having been on parole at Thame, he escaped in March 1811, but was retaken and put on board a prison ship. "No application for one who has broken his parole can be successful", Flinders wrote.

In June 1812, in a letter addressed to Felix Roger, Flinders also explained that restrictions had been applied by the English government with regard to the French colonists because of "the improper conduct of several young men who, having been permitted to return to Guadaloupe and Martinique, have been attempting to make insurrections, and otherwise giving much trouble to the government. Thus the thoughtless proceedings of these individuals has done a real injury to numbers of their countrymen". He also informed the young man, furthermore, that his situation – second surgeon in a privateer – precluded him from being placed on parole. But Felix persisted, asking Flinders to make another application on his behalf, which was done, and in February 1813 Flinders was delighted to forward him the Transport Office's reply: "that in consideration of the circumstances stated by you, Mr. Felix Roger will be allowed to proceed to France with the first invalids that may be sent home".

It was a common practice at this time for individuals to make private arrangements to secure the release of a prisoner, in exchange for one of their own. Thus in July, a Colonel Tyler called on Flinders, proposing to secure the exchange of Louis de Chamisso with his son, a prisoner at Verdun. Flinders promised to help, but was again refused. He commented drily, "Bonaparte will not give an English for a Frenchman". Despite the difficulties, Flinders' help was appreciated. In April 1813, Thomi Pitot wrote – along with another request to assist a young Chauvet – that hearts like his helped to "conserver entre les deux nations quelques liens, quelques points de contact au milieu d'une si horrible guerre". The next month brought good news – Flinders learnt at the Transport Office that the prisoners belonging to Mauritius were to be set at liberty. Ribet, Rondineau, and even Geffroy, were all on the list. Flinders immediately addressed a letter to M. Boucherville, and then wrote several others on his behalf, seeking to secure a passage to the island for him, and to deal with his financial concerns. The news must have been a relief for Flinders who had been under great pressure. Both the young man's parents had written to him – and, he later confided to Mme d'Arifat, Mrs Boucherville claimed that he had been entertained in 'a distinguished manner at her house', while Flinders was convinced that he had never laid eyes on her!

Pitot's charm no doubt continued to smooth over any ruffled feathers, or exasperation on both sides – in July 1813, forwarding yet more requests for help on behalf of the droves of young incarcerated French Creoles, Thomi assured his friend, "vous voyez, Mon ami, que vous continuez à être la providence des creoles de nos Isles". Mauritius was a small island and, as Flinders found, practically everyone could claim a line of parentage to at least one of his friends. Thus, Louis de Chamisso was the adoptive son of Mr. Sornay, Edme Berthelot, - on parole at Morton-Hampstead, was a friend of Mr. Curtat, Joseph Ribet was related to the Périchon family, and Felix Roger to Mme Lachaise, and so it went on.

Even with the notification of their release, the troubles of the prisoners – and of Flinders – were not over. As he told Pitot:

All the Creoles, prisoners here, have permission to return to your islands, in consequence of an application from governor Farquhar; but there are very few, I fear, who can profit by it, the expense of a passage being so great. I am trying everything for young Boucherville, as I will thank you to let his father

> know; but he has no money nor can he hear anything of 200
> dollars which his friends told him he would receive: that sum
> besides is not more than half enough.

More scurrying around on Flinders' part produced bills to the
value of £50 for Piémont de Boucherville.

Through 1813 and early 1814 Flinders continued to lobby on
behalf of French prisoners – a M. Charles Louis Lamy, confined
10 years, was one of his new preoccupations – and of those
colonists seeking to return from France to their island. As
Flinders had predicted, the Sauveget family were among them.
Evidently the ladies had not settled well in France: "c'est
vraiement dommage que Madame Sauvejet et ma bonne grande
amie Noémi ne peuvent pas se contenter en France puisque vous
y êtes; mais soupir après son pays natal est une maladie pour
laquelle la raison ne fait rien", wrote Flinders to his friend. He
once again advised M. Sauveget against taking rash decisions:

> il faut deux ans d'expérience avant de bien savoir si l'on aime
> un pays ou non; on s'y habitue graduellement; et il est probable
> que lorsque la permission arrive, les dames seront assez
> indifférentes au changement. Pensez y bien, consultez vos amis,
> et sachez que presque tous les habitans de Maurice cherche à la
> quitter, et tachez d'en savoir la cause.

Flinders nevertheless requested Mme d'Arifat to ask Farquhar to
confirm that he had no objections to the return of the Sauvegets
and warned his friend that it would take 18 months for the
Governor's reply, and would involve a stay in England of 3 to 6
months, and passage costs of at least 300 guineas. Flinders also
wrote his own recommendation for his friend to Mr Penn of the
colonial department, stating that M. Sauveget had property on
the island, and was his intimate acquaintance, and adding an
unusual tribute: "if I were required to point out the most
peaceable, quiet, and orderly man of my acquaintance, I think it
would be him".

In February 1814 Flinders received the long awaited letter
from Governor Farquhar granting permission for Sauveget's
return, together with his wife, two daughters and two servants.

He suggested that his friend take passage with Mr Le Cornu who was then in London with instructions to purchase a ship and cargo for the Pitots. His instructions to Sauveget are revealing of travel arrangements between France to England at the time:

> *If then my dear Sir you have made up your mind to return to Mauritius, these are the steps you must take. Get the permission of your government to embark in the first cartel from Morlaix. If the vessel go to Dartmouth, come to London in the public stage coach; and on arrival take a hackney coach (fiacre) and drive to Sablonnières hotel, Leicester Square; write a note by the two-penny post to let me know, and I will be with you in a few hours and put you into the right way.*

Mr Sauveget was one of the lucky ones. Relations between France and England were difficult, and Flinders regretfully informed Mme d'Arifat that Philippe Desbassayn's efforts to negotiate an exchange of prisoners had failed: "there are now in England sixty thousand French prisoners, and half that number of Englishmen in France; and to have restored so many unfortunate men to their families, would have been to him a delightful reflexion; but affairs have lately changed so much against Bonaparte, who is in want of officers, that our government would not comply with the terms proposed". Flinders himself was placed in a difficult position as he observed in an ironic aside to one of his Isle of France friends:

> *the predicament in which I stand between the two nations is indeed singular: whilst on the one hand I have been unfeelingly persecuted during six years as a dangerous enemy of France, I am on the other considered as desiring to set myself up for the protector of Frenchmen!*

3. De facto business correspondents

A scarcely less onerous task which accrued to Flinders on his return to England, but one which he gladly took on, was that of furthering the business interests there of his Isle of France friends, and particularly for the house of Pitot. His offices in this respect were reciprocated by Charles, Labauve and the Pitots, who managed some small investments made by Flinders on the island before his departure.

The investments dated back to April 1808 when he placed 1,000 piastres in the keeping of Charles Desbassayns, and arose from Flinders' calculations of the possible return on plantation speculations – he was, as Mack has rightly pointed out, "fascinated by finance" [p. 235-6]. At the time the interest paid in Reunion was at 18%, which Desbassayns hoped to obtain for Flinders. However Charles issued a salutary warning: "les habitans ont leur fortune au soleil; [ils] comptent donc sur leur revenus pour payer … et ils ne viennent qu'une fois l'an". Initially, however, all went well for Flinders, and in August 1809, Charles placed the investment, now amounting to 1439 piastres, into coffee. In 1810, Charles mentioned that 15% interest would be achieved on the sum during each of the following three years.

A second investment made by Flinders, the purchase of some cattle, passed, on his departure, into the hands of Labauve. On his return to England, however, and indeed, until the end of his life, Flinders was troubled by lack of funds. As he wrote to Pitot in December 1811, "my income is inadequate to the expense of living in London, where, nevertheless, I must stay till the voyage is published". All the same, Flinders was reluctant to liquidate his assets held on Mauritius and Bourbon, before they gave a good return: "these are two sources to which I look for a future increase to my income; and from the accounts which I receive of them, to recall these sums would be to kill the poule d'or".

The accounts from Charles Desbassayns of the investment were certainly impressive. In November 1812, Charles reported that he had decided to lend Flinders' money at 12% interest to "M Xavier Bellier, that gentleman who married to a sister of Mme Perichon and brother to the Procureur General Imperial of this island". Desbassayns also informed Flinders that he had accrued interest on his capital in the amount of 22% for the first year, 18% the second and 12% in the third, and for succeeding years. Charles calculated the sum due as $2076. In 1814, Charles informed Flinders that part of the money was settled on a mortgage belonging to his brother-in-law M. Auguste Pajot.

Sugar cane: a speculative Mascarene business

It was regrettable that Flinders did not decide to liquidate his assets in 1813 or 1814, when Pitot volunteered to take charge of this for him, for later when the money was needed by Ann, the financial situation of the parties concerned would be found to have greatly altered. Indeed, writing to Labauve in April 1814, after learning that he had sold Le Refuge, and gone to live on his in-laws' estate, Flinders made a prescient remark when commenting on his friend's business interests: "I should rather wish to see you fixed on a plantation free from encumbrances than even at Palma; but you are more speculative than me, and certainly understand the business better; I should prefer Andre's plan of getting on slowly but surely, as being the least liable to be overthrown by unforeseen events". Times were indeed soon to be difficult, and Labauve and the Pitots would be among the many to face bankruptcy – endangering also Flinders' own modest investment.

Always a generous man, Flinders was frustrated at his inability to make handsome gifts to his friends, writing to Pitot, "I have frequently reproached myself for not having made some returns for your many acts of kindness and liberality. I wished to have sent you various publications and books which would have interested and amused you". He made do with sending a newspaper subscription to his friend, and forwarded small gifts whenever he could. He also willingly took on the role of financial intermediary for his Isle of France friends – in February 1813, for example, Felix de Froberville gave him a bill of exchange upon his brother Prosper in the Isle of France, to the value of 1,200 francs. Flinders' commissions were varied, and included the purchase of a harp for Edouard Pitot's wife, which he informed Thomi "has been made expressly for Madame E. Pitot, as near as possible to your instructions, and I anxiously desire may give satisfaction". In March 1814, Pitot had an even more unusual request – his friend Mallac having lost his job, it was decided to establish a printing press on the island, which he could run. Thus Flinders was requested to purchase this item.

Of course, by this time, Flinders was very ill, and indeed had already written to Pitot apologizing for not having been able to execute his commissions with his usual care. Following his death, Ann sought, as best she could, to deal with the outstanding items to be sent to Pitot and with forwarding his various papers entrusted to her late husband's care. She also began to enquire after her husband's investments on the islands, in her anxiety to provide for herself and her daughter. She initially asked Charles Desbassayns, in December 1814, to continue with her investment, and merely to supply her with a yearly account of the same. At the same time, she wrote to Labauve, now residing at Palma, asking him to sell the cattle and remit the proceeds to England. Pitot wrote her a moving letter of condolence in February 1815 and offered the encouraging news that the 1,000 piastres which Flinders had left with Charles Desbassayns had risen in value to 2,441 piastres. Less happily, the copies of Flinder's published *Voyage*, sent for sale to the Isle of France were destroyed, along with a large part of the Pitot's commercial establishment, in the fire of 28-29 September 1815.

The cattle, however, had fallen in value, as the introduction of large herds had lowered the price in the colony. Labauve instead agreed to purchase the cattle himself, and offered to pay $450, although the actual value of the herd had fallen to a third of the price which Flinders himself had paid for them. Ann replied to Thomi Pitot that

> *any addition to my limited income will be very acceptable - My hopes respecting anything being done for me by the Admiralty become daily more weak; the cry for reform & economy is so great, that no additional pensions can at present be granted, & as my dear Husband did not die in battle or in actual service, I understand that I have no particular claim to offer, his hardships, his long imprisonment, his arduous exertions, avail nothing & seem already to be forgotten - the peculiar pressure of the times too makes against the sale of the voyage, so that my prospects of pecuniary aid are still very gloomy.*

No money was forthcoming however, and by mid 1817, having still received no word from Charles Desbassayns as to Flinders' investment there, she addressed Pitot again, requesting him to make enquiries on her behalf. In January 1818, she wrote to M. Desbassayns herself, urging him to "clear up the apparent mystery attending this affair".

Pitot too, heard nothing from Charles but explained to Ann, in April 1818 that "though he has very large and beautiful landed properties he has been obliged to expend lately an immense deal of money to render them fruitful as sugar estates and that having contracted heavy debts for that purpose he will be for 2 or 3 years more very likely unable to pay his most sacred debt to you. Others say that he is so mortgaged that in case of bad success in his crops he will never pay his debts. ... Mr La Bauve is not in a better situation". Flinders' speculations, like so many on the sugar islands, had proved to be highly precarious ones. In December 1818, however, Labauve forwarded $200 of the sum due for the cattle, and Pitot was able to send in addition a bill of

159

exchange for £65 for some copies of the atlas of the voyage that he had sold.

In 1827, Ann was still waiting for the money due from Charles Desbassayns when he proposed to offer her 5,000 piastres or £1,000 livres sterling. It was revealed that he had placed Flinders' investment with his brother-in-law, Pajot, and had not afterwards been able to realize the sum lent. By now Thomi Pitot had died, and it was Robert Pitot who took over matters on her behalf. The Pitots decided to instruct a lawyer to represent Mrs Flinders' interests, who concluded that "un accommodement vaut beaucoup mieux pour elle, qu'un proces de l'issue duquel on pourrait répondre partout ailleurs qu'à Bourbon". The payment of the debt owed by Charles was placed in the hands of Messrs Manes Jeune frères and an initial sum of £100 was paid to Ann. She replied with thanks, stating that she was very pleased to receive it. She must have been glad to be sent further amounts on a regular basis, eventually receiving around £1,200 from the additional instalments due.

However, in 1838 the Pitots announced yet another bankruptcy – that of the Manes house of commerce. The Pitots had for some time passed over her letters in silence, as they explained: "si nous avons differé de vous écrire, c'est que nous avons toujours ésperé que nous pourrions vous annoncer plus tard une amelioration dans les objets dont nous allons vous entretenir". They estimated that the amount outstanding to her was 1489 piastres (they themselves were owed 2580 piastres). Following the bankruptcy, however, Ann received only 45 piastres (£9.0.6d) as total compensation. Robert added "il est douloureux pour vous, Madame, que vous retiriez si peu de chose d'une créance qui, dans l'origine faisait esperer une rentrée passable", but noted that they themselves were even worse off. Labauve's affairs had also not improved, as he told the Pitots:

> vers l'annee 1830, mes creanciers m'ont evincé de toutes mes propriétés, m'ont accablé de frais de saisies tant immobiliaires que mobiliaires, ne m'ont laissé d'abord qu'une petite pension ... l'interêt de cette petite somme ne se trouvait pas suffisant pour

*les besoins de première necessité de ma famille, il a fallu entamer
le capital aujourd'hui reduit à presque rien, en sorte que si je ne
trouve pas à employer mon industrie, j'arriverai à une misère
absolue, en retenant l'indemnité, on m'a laissé la jouissance de
quelques domestiques, jouissance qui se terminera dans 11 mois
et qui alors doublera ou triplera ma misère. Vous n'etes pas
seule à me faire de reclamations. J'ai fait perdre à ma femme, a
mon frère Marc, à d'autres proches parents. Il a été impossible à
mon caractère de chercher à favoriser les personnes qui m'étaient
les plus chères. Quant à Mme Flinders ma dette envers elle
resulte, d'un acte de generosité en faveur de son mari. Je l'avais
aidé à fournir un petit troupeau de vaches que, j'avais soigné et
nourri pendant plusieurs années. A l'epoque de son départ, il
avait tenté vainement de vendre ce troupeau et comme la gale
venait de l'attaquer, personne n'en voulait. Pour rendre service,
je me suis chargé de ce troupeau, en y mettant un prix élevé. A
cette epoque là, je croyais pouvoir perdre ou donner. J'ai perdu
tout ce troupeau et il ne m'en est resté que la dette. Apres tout,
je n'ai rien à vous offrir, mais comme il est dit que la fortune est
une roue qui tourne, d'en bas elle me menera peut être en haut.*

Labauve's outstanding debt to Ann was in the sum of 559
piastres. Again, the Pitots were owed more. However, they
arranged matters so that she only lost 24 piastres from the
amount due to her – Labauve, they pointed out, had lost
everything. A further small payment was sent to Mrs Flinders in
1842, and left with her agent, she having changed address.

The correspondence entered its third generation in 1843, when
Charles Pitot fils wrote to Ann to inform her of the death of his
father, in his 88th year. The Pitots had, through bankruptcy,
death and innumerable adversities, endeavoured to do their best
for Ann Flinders. Matthew, for his part, could not have imagined
that the early 19th century would bring so much upheaval to the
sugar islands, nor that the first decades of English rule should so
far fall short of what the colonists had hoped. But he surely
would not have judged too harshly those of his friends whose
lives were blighted, as his own had been, with financial problems
- often stemming from rash generosities.

Flinders in Mauritius

Renowned at twenty-nine; a crammed career
Behind; proud, noble hopes ahead; he then
Watches seven summers useless waste away,
(Cribbed, cabined and confined at Le Refuge,
Where humane folk with friendly subterfuge
Lightened a tyrant's yoke) until the day
When he at last was ailing homeward sent
Back to his wife and love, to write his book
About his own-renamed fifth continent
(All coasts now traced, where Torres, Tasman, Cook
But glimpsed or charted part) and of this Isle
Where many prospects pleased, and one great man was vile.
P.J. Barnwell

Conclusion

The events of this book unfolded at a tumultuous time in history which increasingly made its presence felt on the Isle of France. While the forays of Flinders into the island's idyllic interior, his musical soirées, and thé dansantes, at times made the reality of war seem remote, as the blockading squadron tightened its grip on the island, cutting off outside communication and all-important food supplies, the colonists and their celebrated prisoners alike became hostages of war. Flinders, perhaps more than any other English POW of his generation on the island, was well placed to appreciate the concerns of the French inhabitants, and the survival of so many of his letters and diaries provides a unique insight into his reception by them, and, in turn, his perception of Creole society, and reciprocation of the kindness and generosity he was shown.

Flinders was very aware of the debt of gratitude he owed to the inhabitants of Mauritius. As he wrote in a letter to his wife, dated 20th January 1808:

> *the marks of interest which I receive from the inhabitants of this island become daily more extensive, and I receive them even from people who are in intimacy with the general. Any news which seems to announce an approaching peace is communicated to me, directly or indirectly, by several different hands, and I believe when the epoch of my liberation shall arrive, it will excite as much pleasure as many events of much more importance.*

At the same time, he did not feel himself to be an undeserving candidate for their attentions. Shortly after arriving to stay with the d'Arifats at Le Refuge, he remarked in his journal:

> *Madame and her amiable daughters said much to console me, and seemed to take it upon themselves to dissipate my chagrin, by engaging me in innocent amusements and agreeable conversation. - I cannot enough be grateful to them for such kindness, to a stranger, to a foreigner, to an enemy of their*

163

country for such they have a right to consider me if they will, though I am an enemy to no country in fact, but as it opposed the honour, interest and happiness of my own. My employments and inclinations lead to the extension of happiness and of science, and not to the destruction of mankind.

Flinders clearly believed in the humanitarian nature of his life's work, and despite his naval career, was in no sense a bellicose man. He demonstrated an extraordinary capacity to maintain his identity as a patriotic Englishman, whilst immersing himself in the French Creole culture and society that had welcomed him to its bosom. His position was clearly stated in a letter to Thomas Franklin, dated July 6th 1806:

I am indeed, at this time unfortunate, but my misfortunes have made me more friends than enemies, even here, amongst a people inimical to my country; and yet I have not sacrificed or ceased to maintain its honour or interests in order to join that friendship.

This was a quality that he shared with his friend, Thomi Pitot, and perhaps goes some way to explaining the unshakeable foundation of their friendship – both were men firmly committed to their respective nations, and yet never wavered in their understanding that the rights and dignity of their fellow man should always be respected. In one of his many tributes to Pitot, Flinders wrote, "to this excellent man it was, that I was indebted for many services … his exertions ever rose with the occasion that demanded then, and exceeded my desires".

In 1808, when he was planning to escape from the island, Flinders drafted a farewell letter to Thomi, which was never sent. In it, the Englishman offered an honest appraisal of his situation:

I assure you in the sincerity of friendship, that I never did entertain any hostile intention in coming to the Isle of France, nor do I now entertain any in quitting it; on the contrary, I have searched to employ my small means in favour of every honest man in misfortune of whatever nation, and certainly the friendship and kindness I have received during four years from every individual inhabitant of the island with whom I had the honour to be acquainted, has not tended to change my disposition in that respect towards Frenchmen; for you my very dear and worthy friend, and two or three others, I shall cherish a lasting esteem, and in all cases where I may have it in my power to be useful to you, I pray you to count as assuredly upon my services as upon those of an affectionate brother.

In this respect, it is clear that the inhabitants' kindness to English prisoners went far towards ensuring that their own treatment at the hands of their British conquerors would be fair and just. Both Flinders and Owen affirmed that they sought to convince the invading force of the necessity to send a large contingent of troops to capture the Isle of France – so as to procure for the colonists the means to achieve a speedy, yet honorable capitulation. There has been much speculation among historians as to the extent to which Flinders used his knowledge of the island to assist their captors. In fact, he was only one of many prisoners who had information to offer to the English, and if he influenced the course of events in any way, it was rather in the direction of conveying a just appreciation of their fears and concerns – for example with regard to their slaves.

A faction of the French inhabitants, headed by Adrien d'Epinay, perhaps seeking a scapegoat for their fall to the English, later accused Flinders of spying. In his *Simples renseignements sur l'île de France*, d'Epinay claimed that Flinders made soundings along the coast at night, which he transmitted to Bengal. However, records of the British expeditionary force indicate that the cruising ships – notably the officers aboard the *Nisus* – took numerous depth soundings around Mapou bay just prior to the disembarkation. In reality, there was a great deal of information available – the blockading squadron had ample opportunity to survey the coasts, and Flinders himself states that he spent time at the Cape, improving upon the 'rough maps of the port drawn by other naval officers.' The clamour for recognition in the aftermath of the attack – with numerous individuals claiming to have provided *the* crucial piece of intelligence, demonstrates that there was no shortage of information. The fact that Flinders was closely allied to the

165

Pitots – staunch French patriots – and his location in central Vacoas, may actually have made it less rather than more likely that he would have been called upon to pass on sensitive information, while at the Isle of France. And the timing of his departure was too late to have been of any import in the planning of the expedition. He no doubt gave his opinions, which were listened to, but he was ultimately a very small cog in a very large war machine, and his role was negligible at best. More intriguing is the timing of Flinders' release by Decaen and the contention that Hope negotiated his freedom in return for Decaen's own in the event of a capitulation, as has been suggested [Brown: 409]. This has not yet been satisfactorily proved.

The justice of Decaen's actions, and the motivations for holding Flinders has been fully discussed in other works. With the benefit of hindsight, recent studies have tended to criticize Flinders for his initial haughty stance vis-à-vis the French Captain-General, and attempt to assess dispassionately the reasons Decaen may have felt it necessary to retain his English prisoner on the island, long after his release was ordered by Napoleon himself. Flinders' own comment, on the affair, to Captain Bergeret, however, remains compelling. Writing in August 1808, a year or more after those orders were issued, Flinders speculated as to the failure to set him at liberty:

I am lost in conjecture as to the cause, and can only fix myself upon the implacable animosity which the general bears me, and which proceeds to such a length as to make him lay aside even the orders of his government; for from the bottom of my heart I say, that to have refused dining with a general who the day before had qualified me with the title of impostor, is, from all that I know the principal, if not the only cause: he cannot really believe, that it is in my power or intention, or ever was, to do injury to the Isle of France.

The navigator also negated the view that his continued captivity could be because he was a danger to the island, pointing out that other English prisoners of war were released, who knew as much as he did:

*A French cartel is preparing to carry all the English prisoners
in the island, me excepted, to the Cape of Good Hope.
Amongst them are captains Woolcombe and H. Lynne of the
navy, who have been in this island near a year, and know the
port infinitely better than me.*

Another source of speculation surrounding Flinders concerns
the effect of the long detention at the Isle of France upon his
health. Early biographers asserted that his years of imprisonment
hastened his demise. The brief notice on Flinders which
appeared in the *Naval Chronicle* of 1814, for example, attributes
his death to "an organic disease of a chronical character,
engendered no doubt by the early hardships of his professional
life; aggravated by the pestilential tyranny of Buonaparte's
satellite". This view was perpetuated by Ann, who attributed her
husband's death to "a complaint in the bladder, the foundation
of which was no doubt laid during his confinement in the Isle of
France". The reasoning is evident – to establish this principle
would increase the chance of pecuniary compensation – perhaps
in the form of a pension, for Ann.

Flinders himself was not above speculating that his unjust
detention might bring its own reward. In a letter to Thomas
Franklin he wrote:

*I know not what will be the result of the unjust and illiberal
inhospitable treatment I have suffered for more now than twelve
months past, but am not without hope that in the end it may
turn out to my advantage. The imprisonment of an officer
employed on public service, to whom a passport has been given
which he has not violated, is a national insult to our country
and a breach of faith on the part of the French: should it be
taken up in this point of view, the consequence must be that a
recompence for my loss and suffering, and the whole transaction
will, as I hope, redound to my honour.*

Similarly, in a letter to his brother Samuel, dated 6th December
1806, Flinders expressed the view: "I ought to be indemnified
for the sufferings, and losses both of time, rank, fortune, and
reputation which I have been made to undergo for the three last

years". And when Flinders attained post rank on 7th May 1810 this was considered, by a fellow officer, as "a small compensation for unjust detention in the Isle of France, and all your consequent sufferings".

Flinders must certainly have enjoyed the modest measure of notoriety which his detention brought him: in 1811 the celebrated William Wilberforce granted him an audience, wishing to support, "a man who has suffered cruel and most unmerited hardships in his country's cause". However it was spurious to claim that his imprisonment hastened his death – the reality was a lot more uncomfortable – complications from a venereal infection picked up in Tahiti around 1792 is the consensus of opinion concerning his fatal illness today [Ingleton: 455; Brunton: 9].

Certainly, Flinders' descendants had no wish to denigrate the island's inhabitants on account of their famous ancestor. In 1899, his only grandson, W.M. Flinders Petrie, took pains to repudiate such aspersions, informing a Mauritian journalist:

I was brought up to reverence the name of Pitot as that of the kindest and most noble of friends. Whatever the harshness and injustice of the Napoleonic despotism was; yet in the family of Mr Pitot, my grand father found every alleviation that private friendship could afford.

This narrative has sought to stress, indeed, the positive aspects of Flinders' detention: the lessons he learnt from his years in exile, and the friendships he forged. His story has elements of humour, as well as of frustration, and many examples of unlooked-for kindness, as well as mysterious victimization. Flinders himself was aware of the exoticism of his situation, and of its marketability. In an amusing letter to his half-sister, he made the most of his remarkable travels and their denouement:

This letter being written from an island of Africa, on the south side of the equator, by one prisoner man who has three times made the voyage round the world, and seen all manner of things,

sea fights, shipwrecks, and the anthrophagi, it is to be considered
as a curiosity.

He learnt much from his exile, not only in the practical acquisition of the French language, and other local knowledge, but in the less tangible qualities which adversity can bestow. As he confided to his wife, in 1808: "to know how deeply the love of our country and family are engrafted in the human heart, it is necessary to be kept some years from them". And through his journals and letters, he passed on his insights to future generations. His discussions of Creole politics and society are full of interesting vignettes of life in an 18th century French island – already indianized to the extent that the French families habitually eat 'carri', and fully Creolized as his delightful renditions of conversations with the inhabitants reveal. He quotes one resident as telling him, "vous autres Anglais, vous êtes si patriotes que rien ne compte quand il s'agit de l'honneur ou de l'interêt de votre pays". He provides some amusing examples of the insularity of the Isle of France colonists: "ce diable de Pitt", is a phrase which Flinders hears repeatedly. When he asks one Isle of France resident why he is so violently opposed to Pitt (the then British Prime Minister), he replies "il me ruine, il me tue ... j'aime les choux à la folie, il est cause de la guerre, nous ne pouvons plus en avoir de la graine du Cap, et par conséquent, depuis des années il n'y a ni chou ni choufleur qui vaut un liard dans l'isle, et ce diable de Pitt est cause de tout ca".

The reports of such conversations, also provided Flinders with an interesting illustration of the power of propaganda in such a remote colonial outpost:

in few parts of the world are political discussions made with
more freedom than in the Isle of France, though in none, at least
in Europe, is the press under greater restrictions. It is now 15
months since the battle of Trafalgar, yet I am still told of the 19
sail of the line lost by the English in the gale that succeeded that
action; and when I shew a Steele's List wherein the name and
station of every one of the British ships is given some months

after the battle, they say 'cela ne prouve rien, c'est un fausseté du
Gouvernement Anglais pour mieux cacher leur perte'.

Yet, despite the propaganda efforts of the local government, aided by its partisan press, Flinders could not but be impressed by the number of the islanders who "tried to soften my captivity. They sought to lighten the sorrow and chagrin which from time to time I could not help but feel… Until I left Vacouas in 1810, I had not believed that so many people in the island felt so strongly about the notorious injustice of my long imprisonment. …. This proved that even a strong and national government cannot keep a people from wishing to see men treated in just and humane fashion".

Flinders was aware of the supreme irony of having found so many friends in such inauspicious circumstances. Addressing a letter to Barthelemy de Froberville, in January 1809, he noted, "L'endroit où j'ai éprouvé la plus grande injustice, ou j'ai rencontré un homme manquant de tout bon principe, est aussi celui où, hors de ma propre famille, j'ai trouvé le plus d'amitié, de compassion pour mes infortunes". Perhaps the most significant aspect of this account of one man's exile on the Isle of France, is the lesson men like Flinders and Pitot imparted – that it is possible to combine a strong sense of national loyalty with the recognition that those, even of diametrically opposed political views, can become close and abiding friends. The last word, naturally, belongs to Flinders himself:

What mixed sensations will the remembrance of the Isle of France excite! The scene of the greatest injustice, the most durable misfortune I ever witnessed, and the same where I found by long experience that the mass of mankind are naturally good and humane. If I know my own heart, the one will be forgiven, and perhaps forgotten; but oh ye worthy and generous inhabitants of Mauritius! who treated me as a brother and felt for my misfortunes as for those of an esteemed friend, can I ever forget or cease to feel the deepest interest in what may concern you? Never but with the annihilation of my faculties.

170

Bibliography

Flinders prepared a narrative of his experiences, kept a journal and made copies of his correspondence in the form of letter books while on the Isle of France. Fortunately his papers were kept safe by his widow Ann until her death in 1852, and thereafter by her daughter and grandson, eventually finding their way into archival collections where they can be seen today.

Primary Sources

1. Journals

During his detention, Flinders kept a Private Journal. This is reproduced as a manuscript facsimile by Geoffrey Ingleton as volume II of his book. Flinders used the journal as the basis for much of the story of his exile described in his *A Voyage to Terra Australis*. The State Library of New South Wales (SLNSW) Australia holds the original, while the Public Record Office (PRO) London, has a copy of Flinder's Narrative in the Admiralty series, and a fragment can be found amongst Flinders' papers in the National Maritime Museum (NMM) at Greenwich.

2. Letters

Collections of the letters of Flinders have been published by Brunton, Hill and Retter & Sinclair among others. The largest collection of letters by Flinders is held by the SLNSW, in the form of his Private and Public Letter Books. The NMM has a good collection of original letters from Flinders' correspondents. Some letters of Thomi Pitot are housed in the Carnegie Library, Mauritius, with a typed copy in the Mauritius Archives. A number of letters addressed by Flinders to government departments – particularly concerning French prisoners of war - is disseminated in Admiralty and Colonial Office files held in the Public Record Office.

Secondary Sources

Archer, Kirstie 'Mapping terra incognita' *Lancet* 358, no. 9299, 2001, p. 2180-2181

Austen, H.C.M. *Seafights and Corsairs of the Indian Ocean, being the Naval History of Mauritius from 1715 to 1810*, R W Brooks, Port Louis, 1935

Auzoux, A. 'l'Arrestation du Capitaine Flinders', *Revue d'Histoire Diplomatique*, vol. 26, 1912 p 480-515

Baker, S.J. *My Own Destroyer*, Angus & Robertson, Sydney, 1963

Barnwell, P.J. ed. 'Flinders and Mauritius' *Bulletin de la Société de l'Histoire de l'Ile Maurice* Vol II 1939-1944, p 3-43

Barnwell, P.J. 'Poetic homage to Flinders' *Bulletin de la Société de l'Histoire de l'Ile Maurice* Vol III 1939-1944, p. 57

Beard, W. *Navigator Immortal. The Life and Adventures of Matthew Flinders*, Glebe, 1958

Bidwell, S. *Swords for Hire: European Mercenaries in 18th Century India*, John Murray, London, 1971

Brown, A.J. *Ill-starred Captains. Flinders and Baudin*, Chatham, London, 2001

Brunton, P. ed. *Matthew Flinders personal letters from an extraordinary life*, Hordern House, Australia, 2002

Bryant, J. *Captain Matthew Flinders. His Voyages, Discoveries and Fortunes*, London 1928

Burrows, E.H. *Captain Owen of the African Survey*, A.A. Balkema, Rotterdam, 1979

Cannon M. *The Exploration of Australia*, Sydney: Readers' Digest Services Pty Ltd, 1987

Carter, Paul "Plotting: Australia's Explorer Narratives as 'Spatial History'" *Yale Journal of Criticism*, vol 3, no 2, 1990

Compton, H. *A Particular Account of the European Military Adventurers of Hindustan 1784-1803*, London Fisher Unwin, 1893

Defos du Rau, J. *L'Ile de la Réunion, Etude de géographie humaine*, Bordeaux, 1960

Dictionnaire de Biographie Mauricienne, SHIM, Mauritius, issues from 1941 to present.

Dudding, Sir J. *Captain Matthew Flinders RN His life and place in the exploration of Australia*, 1974

Finkel, G. *Matthew Flinders*, Collins, Sydney, 1973

Flinders, M. *A Voyage to Terra Australis*, London, 1814, Australiana Facsimile Editions, 1966

Flinders, M. *Trim*, Collins, Sydney, 1977

Hill, E. *My Love Must Wait*, Lloyd O'Neil, Australia 1971

Ly Tio Fane Pineo, H. *In the grips of the Eagle. Matthew Flinders at Ile de France, 1803-1810*, MGI, Mauritius, 1988

Mack, J.D. *Matthew Flinders, 1774-1814*, Nelson, 1966

McMaster, J. B. *The Life and Times of Stephen Girard, Mariner and Merchant*, Lippincott, Philadelphia, 2 vols 1918

Mellick, S.A. 'John White and Matthew Flinders, Voyageurs Aventureux in New South Wales 1788–1799' *Aust. N.Z. J. Surg.* (2000) 70, 875–882

Prudhomme, C. *Histoire religieuse de la Réunion*, Karthala, 1984

Retter, C. & Sinclair, S. *Letters to Ann. The Love Story of Matthew Flinders and Ann Chappelle*, Angus & Robertson, Sydney, 1999

Rouvier, C. *Histoire des Marins Français 1789-1808*, Paris

Scott, E. *The Life of Captain Matthew Flinders*, Sydney, Angus & Robertson, 1914

State Library of New South Wales *Matthew Flinders. The Ultimate Voyage*, 2001

Taylor, V. *Two families of Ile de France - de Chazal and Rouillard*, Private publication, 1985.

Toussaint, A. *Histoire des Iles Mascareignes, Eds. Berger-Levrault*, Paris, 1972

Toussaint, A. *Le Mirage des Iles Le négoce français aux Mascareignes au XVIIIe siècle*, Edisud, France, 1977

Toussaint, A. 'Liste des négociants ayant exercé à l'Ile de France au XVIIIe siècle, *Bull. de la Société de l'Histoire de l'Ile Maurice*, 1988

Wildes, H.E. *Lonely Midas: the Story of Stephen Girard*, Farrar & Rinehart, New York, 1953.

Biographies

Airolles, Joseph – *resided on Mesnil, where the former estate of La Pérouse was situated. He married Anne Chasteigner Paradis in Plaines Wilhems in 1801 and was widowed in 1808. His wife's daughters were married to Bickham, Chazal and Chevreau, all friends of Flinders.*

Aken, John – *master of the Investigator, also sailed with Flinders in the Cumberland and was imprisoned on Mauritius with him. He left the island aboard the American ship James on 20 May 1805.*

Barbé de Marbois, Claude François Nicolas – *settled on the island from France, and became a senior judge. He was a friend of M. Curtat, through whom Flinders secured an introduction. Claude was the younger brother of the Marquis François de Barbé-Marbois who held an important political post in France, and was therefore solicited by Flinders to write a letter on his behalf to the Marquis. Flinders also reported that Barbé de Marbois was wounded in a duel with Augustin Baudin. Barbé de Marbois married 3 times, but had no children. He died in 1830.*

Barbé Laurent Gabriel Lovis – *merchant and formerly officer in the merchant marine, born in Brittany in 1766. He married Adelaide, the daughter of Jean Nicolas Céré in 1772. He commanded a corps of the National Guard during the English conquest and spent his last years in France where he died in 1846.*

Baudin, Nicolas – *born in 1754, he joined the French navy in 1774, and made several scientific voyages, notably a survey of the coast of Australia with two ships, Le Géographe and Le Naturaliste. He met Flinders at Encounter Bay in April 1802, and, stopping at Mauritius in1803, died there in September. His brother,* **Augustin Baudin**, *who commanded a merchant ship in the service of the Danish settlement at Tranquebar, India, met Flinders at the Isle of France, and asked his advice about taking* **Mary Beckwith** - *an ex-convict who had travelled with Nicolas Baudin from Sydney - to India.*

Baudin, Charles – *born in 1784, he embarked as a midshipman in the Géographe in 1800 and was promoted to ensign in 1804. He spent time at the Isle of France in between missions, and while recuperating from injuries sustained in combat in 1808, where he became a friend of Matthew Flinders. He was promoted to post captain in 1814, and later to admiral. He died in Paris in 1854.*

Bayard, Antoine – *appointed a judge by General Decaen in 1803, he was introduced to Flinders by his friend Pitot. He lost his post on account of his deafness, soon after the British conquest and died at Flacq in 1820.*

Bergeret, Jacques – *born at Bayonne in 1751, he entered the navy in 1792 and was a captain by 1796, when he distinguished himself in the Virginie in a battle with a superior Enlish force. He arrived at the Isle of France in 1802 and commanded a corsair until it was purchased by Decaen, and he was gien the command. He was taken prisoner in 1805, but returned to the Isle of France in the same year. He returned, shortly afterwards to France, and eventually became an admiral and a senator. He died at Paris in 1857.*

Bickham, Martin – *born into a New Jersey Quaker family, Martin Bickham was brought up in the household of wealthy French-American merchant Stephen Girard, and came to Mauritius on the Sally brig as a supercargo in 1798. He married a daughter of Mme Airolles – Ramona Eugenia Rivalz - and thereby became a member of the social circle also frequented by Flinders on Mauritius. American shipping was an important conduit for Flinders' letters and as a departure route for English POWs, and the two consequently were in contact on many occasions. Bickham acted as American Consul at the Isle of France between 1816-1825.*

Boand, Johann – *a Swiss mercantile agent. for the house of Portalis at Neufchatel who befriended Flinders.*

Bonnefoy, François Dominique – *acted as interpreter while Flinders was in Port Louis. He had arrived in Mauritius in 1775 on La Natalie, and is listed in the Port Louis census as a 35 year old in 1796. He died in 1823.*

Boucherville, Louis René Boucher de – *born in Montreal in 1736, of a French lineage settled in Canada since the 17th century, he spent some time in England as a POW, and refused to return to Canada under British rule, despite losing his property there. Instead he joined the Isle of France regiment, and there married Catherine Drouet in 1776. He took part in Indian campaigns, before settling at Wolmar, Black River, where he died in 1825. His son,* **Piémont de Boucherville,** *also a POW in England, was assisted by Flinders.*

Cabot, John Higginson – *born into a Massachusetts trading family in 1782, he acted as agent at the Isle of France for Salem merchants where he met Flinders. His relative,* **Andrew Cabot,** *also visited the island.*

Cap-Martin, M. – *a former French naval officer, who sailed on the Géographe with Nicolas Baudin, and settled in Mauritius after marrying into the Perichon family. He died in October 1809.*

Charrington, Edward – *of Deptford joined the Investigator in 1801, as a 23 year old able seaman, and later served as boatswain. Sailed in the Cumberland with Flinders and consequently was imprisoned on the Isle of France along with* **George Alder, Henry Lewis, William Smith, John Elder** *who served as Flinders' servant and* **John Wood.** *They all left the Isle of France before Flinders.*

Chazal, Toussaint Antoine de – *born at Port Louis in 1770, in 1787 he left for France with his brother to complete his education, but was briefly imprisoned. He purchased the estate of Mondrain with his brother in 1796, and was Flinders' neighbour, together with his wife* **Charlotte Juliette Anne Laurence Rivalz de Saint Antoine** *whom he married in 1799. They had six children. An accomplished artist, his portrait of Flinders is well known. A friend of Governor Farquhar, he died in 1822 at Reduit, reportedly of an overdose of opium. His estate of was between Henrietta and the Trois Mamelles.*

Chevreau, Pierre Paulin – *born at Port Louis in 1774, he married Louise Rivaltz de Saint-Antoine, and was a neighbour of Flinders at Le*

177

Refuge. He died in 1831 and his wife in 1859. His sister **Mme Lachenardière***, also met Flinders and introduced him to her friend Madame St. Suzanne, the wife of* **Colonel C. Bruneteau de Sainte-Suzanne***, a military officer who arrived with Decaen in 1803. In 1805 he was named Colonel of the Isle of France Regimen, and in 1809 he succeeded des Bruslys as Commandant of Bourbon, overseeing the handover to the English on 9th July 1810.*

Couve, Antoine *– a merchant of Montpellier, he arrived to join his brothers Jean-Baptiste and Philippe at the Isle of France in 1790, and became a notable there. Flinders enjoyed many visits to his residence, and found his daughters charming. One of them later married Augustin Gourel de St Pern. He was less enamoured of Philippe Couve, who visited him briefly in London.*

Curtat, Jean Antoine Louis *– a Swiss-born lawyer and friend of Flinders, he came to the Isle of France in 1786. He was the owner of the Clarens estate at Tamarin in the Isle of France which Flinders visited, and died at Port Louis in 1825, aged 67. His nephew* **Edouard Ossère** *was one of the prisoners of war whom Flinders assisted in England.*

Dale, Alfred *– midshipman, captured aboard the Dedaigneuse by the French and brought to Mauritius, where he met Flinders at the Garden Prison. He assisted Flinders with his charts before his release in July 1805.*

d'Arifat, Mme Louise Geneviève *– née Deribes, and born in 1758, the daughter of the island's procureur-general and a member of the Conseil Supérieur. She married Marc de la Bauve d'Arifat at Moka, a major in the Isle of France regiment in 1777 and was widowed in 1799. Flinders' hostess at Le Refuge, Mme d'Arifat died on her son's estate at Black River on 10 Aug 1812. Her eldest daughter,* **Delphine Louise Antoinette Marie***, was born at Moka on 26 March 1783, and married M. Pailleux, a Parisian residing in Bourbon. She died there in 1875. A second daughter,* **Louise Sophie***, born in 1792, married Charles Desbassayns, in 1808, at the age of 15. Of her sons,* **André** *was married and already lived at Flacq, when Flinders was at Le Refuge; he taught the two younger sons,*

Marc *and* **Aristide**, *and became friendly with* **Labauve**, *who was closer to him in age, and who later married* **Delphine Perichon**.

Decaen, Charles Mathieu Isidore – *Flinders' nemesis, this army officer turned colonial governor was offended by the Englishman's haughty behaviour on his arrival at the Isle of France, and, while justified in his initial suspicions, prolonged Flinders' incarceration beyond that of any other POW under his jurisdiction. He arranged a favourable capitulation for himself, his troops and the colonists in 1810, and returned to France, carrying Flinders' journal with him. He died in 1832.*

Deglos, Jacques Armand – *a merchant from Honfleur, he came to the Isle of France in 1800 and was resident in Port Louis, where he met Flinders, around 1804. He subsequently purchased several items for the Englishman during his trips to India. He died on 1st August 1816. His relative, Jean Stanislas Victor Deglos, was a merchant captain who subsequently became a corsair and married a niece of Charles Pitot in 1801, hence the family connection which led to the introduction of Jacques Deglos to Flinders. Jean died in 1811, and Jacques in 1816.*

Desbassayns, Charles André – *born in 1782 at St Paul, Bourbon, the son of Henri Paulin Panon Desbassayns and Ombline Gonneau Montbrun, the largest landed proprietors of that island. His father Henri was an astute businessman who protected himself against the risks of revolutionary France by placing an important part of his revenues in the United States – at Boston. The family spent some time in America, to escape the Revolution, and educated the boys there. Charles' father died in 1800, but his mother continued to administer the family fortunes. Charles and his brother Joseph were the first to take advantage of the commercial opportunities offered by sugar production in Réunion. The owner of two large estates on that island, Charles married* **Louise Sophie de Labauve d'Arifat** *on 21st January 1808 in the presence of Matthew Flinders. Charles became a good friend of the navigator, and named his first son* **Henry François Flinders Panon Desbassayns** *in his honour. Unfortunately, the boy, born in 1811, died young on 3rd March 1818. Charles and his wife had 8 children, of whom 4 reached adulthood. Flinders invested 1,000 piastres with Charles, but after his death, Ann experienced* much difficulty in obtaining the sum, and the interest due. Charles had a brilliant career in Bourbon, and died at the age of 85, in 1863; his wife lived until 1874. Charles' brothers Henri, Panon and Philippe were also known to Flinders. **Philippe Panon Desbassayns, Comte de Richemont**, was sent to France for his studies as a six year old boy, and subsequently held a number of diplomatic posts in France, in the course of which he visited England on several occasions, where he met Flinders and offered to intercede on his behalf with the French authorities, to obtain his journal and the lifting of his parole. His brother, **Henry-Charles Panon Desbassayns de Montbrun** and his wife Anne, spent most of the year 1813 in London where they socialized frequently with Matthew and Ann Flinders.

D'Unienville, Marie Claude Antoine, Baron – born in 1766, he served in the French navy with Saint-Felix before settling on the island, where he married three times. Appointed Major of the district of Savanne, he was the first officer to meet Flinders from the Cumberland. He was appointed Colonial Archivist in 1813.

Exshaw, John – born in Ireland, he married into the French-Creole Kerbalanec family and consequently socialized with Flinders on the Isle of France. He travelled frequently on business and also met Flinders in London, after the latter's return to England.

Foisy, Jacques Nicolas – born in Paris, and a lawyer by profession, he came to the Isle of France in 1786, where he married a Creole, Marie Cecile Drouet. His daughter **Felicité Clementine**, born in 1795, had a brief and tragic love affair with a young English naval lieutenant, Archibald Litchfeld. She died at the age of 45 in 1804.

Hamelin, Jacques Félix Emmanuel – a French naval officer and acquaintance of Flinders having commanded Le Naturaliste, consort of Nicolas Baudin's Géographe. (1768-1839) Born in 1768, he served in the merchant marine before joining the navy in 1792. In 1808 he took command of the Venus, his duties including the protection of Isle of France shipping. He became a rear admiral and a baron in 1811, and died in Paris, in 1839.

Henry, Captain – *and his wife were at the Garden Prison with Flinders before their release. They continued to correspond after Henry's departure. Henry was later promoted to Major.*

Hope, Hugh – *arrived in Mauritius in December 1809 as commissary of prisoners aboard the Harriet cartel of which John Ramsden was the commander. He negotiated with Decaen for Flinders' release, and his successful 'mission' was duly recompensed in India. He continued to correspond with Flinders after his departure from the island.*

Huet de Froberville, Barthélemy – *soldier and prolific writer, born in 1761 in France. He was the author of Sidner, the first novel to be published on the island, a founder member of the Société d'Emulation Intellectuelle and editor of the voyages of Mayeur to Madagascar in 10 volumes. Flinders visited his residence at Moka on several occasions. His son* **Jacques Felix de Froberville** *(with whom he is confused by Brunton and other authors) was born at Port Louis in 1789 and joined the French navy at a young age, serving on the Venus with Hamelin. He was a prisoner first at the Cape and then in England, where Flinders worked to secure his release.*

Kerjean, Colonel Joseph Jacques Xavier Marie Desnos de – *born on the island in 1754, he served in the Pondicherry Regiment. Briefly imprisoned in Revolutionary France, he came back to the Isle of France from Tranquebar in 1804, and returned there in 1806. He died at Brest in 1821. He was one of a number of military officers praised by Flinders for their consideration towards English prisoners.*

la Pérouse, Jean François de Galaup, Comte de – *celebrated French explorer, born 22 Aug 1741, lived in the Isle of France from 1771 to 1778, killed in the South Seas, 1788.*

Larkins, Thomas – *he commanded the Warren Hastings, an East Indiaman captured by La Piémontaise in June 1806 and was brought to Mauritius as a prisoner. He corresponded with Flinders while on the island and carried Flinders' narrative and letters with him to England.*

Linois, Charles Alexandre Léon Durand de – *another of Flinders' correspondents, who wrote a letter in his behalf, Linois was born in 1761 into a noble Breton family, and joined the navy as a young man, serving with Suffren and St Félix. Admiral Linois was taken prisoner in 1806, and spent 8 years in England. However he was granted parole, and made a Count of the Empire by Napoleon. After his return to France in 1814 he was appointed Governor of Guadeloupe. He died in 1848.*

Mallac, Jacques – *from Bordeaux, he came to the island in 1803, occupied several legal positions and married twice. He was one of the founder members – in 1805 – of the literary society La Table Ovale, and of a literary review. Flinders describes him as a good raconteur.*

Moncamp, Paul Martin – *born in 1758, he was educated at Geneva and in Paris where he studied medicine. His language skills led to his selection for a diplomatic mission amongst the Indian Princes. He came to the island in 1788 and settle at Trianon in Plaines Wilhems, where he socialized with Flinders. He died on his estate in 1827. He was very close to Decaen, and corresponded with him after the General left the island.*

Monistrol, Colonel Louis Augustin Fulcher de – *born at Loreient in 1774 he embarked on a military career in 1789 and was posted to the Isle of France in 1803. On the arrival of Matthew Flinders, in December of that year, he was ordered to examine the navigator's papers, and effectively became Decaen's intermediary with Flinders. He returned to France after the British conquest, where he continued his military career, and died in Paris in 1849.*

Owen, William Fitzwilliam – *born in 1774, he entered the navy in 1788, and served with Pellew. He was brought to the Isle of France as a prisoner in December 1808, and left on the Harriet, with Flinders in 1810. He supplied information to the expeditionary force against the Isles of France and Bourbon, and superintended the transports, but left to rejoin his ship before the final assault. He subsequently became a naval hydrographer of some importance and is chiefly remembered for his surveys of the North American lakes and coastline. He died in Canada in 1857.*

Pelgrom, Charles de - *trader and consular agent, probably born into an Austrian noble family, visited Flinders in Port Louis and facilitated several transactions for him. Pelgrom arrived at the island in 1782 and was engaged in commerce there from 1784. In 1799 he was named Consul for Denmark at a time when trade between the island and the Danish settlements in India (at Tranquebar and Bengal) was flourishing. In 1805 he departed for Europe on business, returning in 1807.*

Perichon de Beauplan, Jean Marie – *born in Paris, he served in the military and was posted to the Isle of France regiment in 1780. He was one of the colonists who refused to swear the oath of allegiance, and returned to Morlaix in France. He died in Bourbon in 1792.*

Pitot, Charles Thomi – *a businessman and politician, born 8 November 1779 and died on 23 May 1821. He is buried at Pamplemousses. Pitot was Flinders' closest friend on Mauritius, and a man whose many kindnesses were testified to by other English prisoners. During Farquhar's governorship of the island, Thomi was the de facto leader of the French Mauritians. His sister,* **Marie Françoise Pitot** *married* **Jean François Michel Rouillard** *of St Malo in 1787. They settled in Poudre d'Or and had seven children. One of their daughters, Clémence, (Flinders called her Clementina) married her uncle,* **Edouard Pitot**. *The couple lived at l'Amitié after 1819, and had 6 children together. Edouard is well known as an artist. A second sister,* **Jeanne Pitot** *married* **Xavier Brunet** *in 1792. Mme Brunet was later captured in the Marquess Wellesley cartel and complained bitterly of her treatment to Flinders.*

Plumet, Jacques – *a former military officer, who had served under the Mahratta rulers in India, notably in two battles of June and July 1801. He left their service shortly thereafter and settled on the Isle of France. He had a fine 400-acre plantation near Moka, which Flinders visited.*

Robertson, Walter – *surgeon in the employment of the Government of Bengal, and fellow prisoner of Flinders at the Maison Despeaux.*

Saint Felix, Armand Philippe Germain, Marquis de – *during his long naval career, served with the legendary Suffren, and in the Indian Ocean where he made an enemy of the Jacobin faction on the Isle of France and was briefly imprisoned. In 1793 he purchased a property at Plaines Saint Pierre in Black River district and lived there with his wife and children between 1795 and 1810, where he was one of the many acquaintances of Flinders.*

Saulnier, Jacques Nicolas – *arrived with his brother Jean Jacques at the island in 1788, where they both married and settled, as merchants and landowners. Jacques Nicolas resided in Port Louis, and it is probably he who visited Flinders at the Garden Prison, although the Englishman knew both families.*

Sauveget, Jean Baptiste – *of Lorraine, France, a merchant. He came to the Isle of France in 1788 and married Petronille Vignol there in 1794. Flinders knew the family well, and visited their home at Rivière Latanier on several occasions; he was particularly fond of their daughter, Noémie. He assisted them to return to the Isle of France shortly after the British conquest, but Sauveget appears to have returned definitively to France in 1817, dying at Paris in 1854.*

Translations

185

p. 52   *"il faut faire... cette isle!"*
          - every sacrifice possible, I believe must be made – you must get out of this island!

p. 52-3   *"ce qui me plait .... ma femme"*
          - what pleases me the most, with regard to the Anglicization of the two islands is 1) that your communication with Mr and Mrs Desbassayns will no longer be interrupted by the war and 2) that I will see my dear friends again ... within 2 years, perhaps with my wife.

p. 53   *"Ce changement ... son jugement"*
          - This change could open up career possibilities to my young friends Aristide and Marc ... commerce will be re-established with India, and will employ many ships, on one of which Aristide or his brother could take employment, and if it suits him, when I arrive, I would propose to him to undertake a voyage of discovery with me, and assuming the islands remain English at the peace, the Royal Navy would be open to him, or he could abandon the idea according to his circumstances and to his judgment.

          "il est possible que ... en France"
          - it is possible that the event about to occur at your island will encourage your desire to return to France, in that case... I renew the offer of my assistance, either in England or to speed up your passage to France.

          "un officier distingué et d'un mérite reconnu"
          - a distinguished officer of recognized merit.

p. 56   *"jamais, mon cher ..... être sans elle"*
          - never, my dear Mr Sauveget, will we find a second Mrs d'Arifat. She was the most perfect model of all that is good and estimable among mankind, and Heaven could no longer do without her.

p. 56   *"qui par ses connaissances .. avec succès"*
- who, through his acquaintance with, and services rendered, to the great and good, is in a suitable position to make the request successfully.

"les colons sont plus .... sans valeur"
- the colonists are happier than they have been for many years, however, land has lost its value.

p. 56   *"Je n'ai jamais cessé ... à la colonie"*
- I have never ceased to have a sincere esteem and attachment for your brother, convinced as I am of his social virtues, talents and devotion to the colony.

p. 71   *"Ce n'est pas pour .... à l'utilité générale"*
- It is not for an Englishman, Sir, that I entreat you: in his capacity as head of an expedition of discovery, Mr Flinders has become the representative of all civilized nations, adopted by all, seen by all as a friend devoted to the welfare and happiness of mankind.

p. 87   *"je desire beaucoup .... commodités et agremens"*
- I hope very much that you find in my little retreat some comforts and conveniences.

p. 94   *"ou entre les bienfaiteurs .... les heros célebrés"*
- either among the benefactors of mankind or among celebrated heroes.

"une femme affectionée ..... mon estime"
- an affectionate wife and an excellent mother. She possesses my highest consideration and my esteem".

p. 98   *"à manger un carrie dans les bois"*
- to eat a curry in the woods.

pertains to the slave trade in England, will influence the worthy judge who will hear our case.

p. 117   *"montre bien …. combat et du résultat"*
- well demonstrates the respect your government has for our skill and the bravery of my compatriots … I await impatiently your account of the battle and the result.

p. 120-1   *"Oh comme je desire … et des sciences"*
- Oh how I wish that all the French and English shared the same views for each other as you and I. Then peace would reign in Europe and we would contest nothing other than friendship, arts and science.

p. 121   *"Ce Brigand ….. d'homme en lethargie"*
- a diatribe against Napoleon by Desbassayns who sighs for the moment when the Good Lord will call the 'Corsican brigand' to him; until then he will keep his political sentiments in check.

p. 123-4   *"la carronade commença… Chef Conspirateur"*
- Desbassayns recounts the English attack on Bourbon – the drunken and disorderly conduct of sailors from the Caroline, the British plans, the inhabitants' unwillingness to fight, the suicide of DesBrulys at Bourbon, and the unleashing of bloody acts sponsored by the sans culottes and their vows of vengeance against Anglophiles, of whom Desbassayns is designated 'Chief Conspirator'.

p. 124   *"oblige moi mon Ami …. je suis chargé"*
- help me, my friend, by transmitting them to me, and they will not be divulged. This knowledge could be very important to my interests.

p. 126   *"que nous serons bientôt compatriotes?"*
- that we will soon be compatriots.

p. 126   *"pour que cela s'accomplisse ... je les ai trouvés"*
- so that blood would not be spilled. I preached the advantage of sending a large force so that the inhabitants would not need to make a futile resistance, I depicted them as tolerant, agreeable and generally good, as I found them.

"cet evenement malheureux .... vous peindre"
- Pitot describes the dishonorable capitulation of Bourbon, but affirms that it strengthens the resolution of the Isle of France colonists to fight and discusses the training programme of the troops there.

p. 126-7 *"de nous fair jetter dans les bras du seduisant Mr Farquhar"*
-to throw us into the arms of the seductive Mr Farquhar.

p. 127   *"tous les debarquements ... champ de bataille"*
- the enemy landings were repulsed by the inhabitants and 250 troops fled from 30 or 40 of our artillery men, leaving their dead strewn over the battlefield.

p. 127-9 *"A 9 heures ... rendent à discretion"*
- a description by Pitot of the famous battle of Grand Port, in which the English, having taken control of the fort on the islet of Ile de la Passe, tempted in French frigates, by raising the French flag and then engaged them in battle. The ships ran aground, and the English ultimately came off worst with heavy casualties to both sides. The English on the islet, with no possibility of obtaining supplies, were also obliged to surrender.

p. 131-32 *"une force considérable ... de la capitulation"*
- Pitot recounts the disembarkation of the English in overwhelming numbers, forcing the colonists to concede defeat. He and his brother Edouard mounted a brief assault on the advancing troops, and Edouard was taken prisoner, while Thomi anxiously searched for him.

p. 132   *"c'est votre pavillon qui flotte ... sains et saufs"*
- it is your flag which flies everywhere over our island. The great event was accomplished without us having to shed a single tear – our relatives and friends are all safe and sound.

p. 132   *"très honorable, très favorable aux habitans"*
- very honourable, very favourable to the inhabitants.

p. 132   *"une parfaite connaissance du caractère et des gouts de Charles"*
- a perfect understanding of the character and tastes of Charles.

p. 136   *"mon fils Aristide ... aux malabards"*
- my son Aristide along with innumerable others has lost his job ... little by little the French are being ousted from their posts to give them to the English, while the more menial jobs are going to the Indians.

p. 139   *"La France est abaissée ... par l'orgueil"*
- France is on its knees; England is at the apogee of her happiness, may your compatriots learn from the dreadful example which the world has been given, how unstable is a power founded on injustice, and exercised by pride.

p. 146   *"vous avez quitté l'expedition ... ses recherches"*
- you left the expedition before it had accomplished its objectives, you did not rejoin when it returned to the Isle of France; your work, however estimable it may be, was not accomplished through the expedition or in the countries with which it was concerned.

p. 149   *"il me peine de savoir ... ce moment"*
- it troubles me to learn that there is another Isle of France Creole prisoner here, and especially when it is not within my power to be useful to him at this time.

p. 152 *"enfin mon cher Monsieur, …bien des bénédictions"*
- in fact, my dear Sir, your manner of dealing with these poor prisoners has showered many blessings upon you.

p. 153 *"conserver entre les … horrible guerre"*
- maintain between the two nations, some ties, some points of contact in the middle of such a horrible war.

"vous voyez, ….creoles de nos Isles"
- you see, my friend, you continue to be a godsend for the Creoles of our islands.

p. 154 *"c'est vraiement dommage …. fait rien"*
- it's a real shame that Mme Sauveget and my good friend Noemi cannot be happy in France, since you are there; but to sigh for one's mother country is a sickness which does not understand reason.

"il faut deux … savoir la cause"
- 2 years of experience are needed before one can know if one likes a country or not, one accommodates to it slowly, and it is probable that by the time the permission arrives, the ladies will be quite indifferent to the change. Think well, consult your friends, be aware that almost all the inhabitants of Mauritius are seeking to leave, and try to find out the reason.

p. 156 *"les habitans ont … une fois l'an"*
- the inhabitants depend on the weather for their profit; and count on their sales - which come only once a year - to pay their debts.

p. 160-1 *"vers l'année 1830 …. En haut"*
Labauve explains that around 1830 all his properties were seized and his own family members lost as a result. That his debt towards Flinders resulted from an act of generosity, and that he has no means to pay, however if

192

the wheel of fortune once again turns his way, it will be his creditors who will benefit.

p. 169 *"vous autres Anglais ... votre pays"*
- you English are so patriotic that nothing counts when the honour or the interest or your country is at stake.

"il me ruine ... tout ça"
- he ruins me, he kills me ... I love cabbages with a passion, and because of the war we can no longer get the seeds from the Cape, with the result that there have been no cabbages or cauliflowers worth a dime in the island, and that devil Pitt is the cause of it all.

p. 170 *"l'endroit où j'ai ... mes infortunes"*
- the place where I suffered the greatest injustice, where I met a man lacking in all principle, is also that where, outside my own family, I found the most friendship and compassion in my misfortune.

A Tribute: Flindesia Australis

*"A tree of moderate size, observed September 1802, both in
flower and with ripe capsules, in the woods and thickets near the
head of Broad Sound, on the East coast of New Holland, in
about 23o S. lat. The examination of Broad Sound was
completed at the same time by Captain Flinders, to
commemorate whose merits I have selected this genus from the
considerable number discovered in the Expedition, of which he
was the able and active commander".*

Brown, Robert General Remarks, Appendix to *Voyage to
Terra Australis*, Vol II, pp 533-613.